SONOS
The Home Sound System

Listen Better
at **sonos.com**

A designer knows he has achieved perfection not when there is nothing left to add, but when there is nothing left to take away.

— Antoine de Saint-Exupery

SØRENSEN

Sorensen. Luxury leather for the most
iconic designs in the world

S
PEAU SØRENSEN LEATHER
PIEL LEDER LÆDER LEDER
19 73

Arctander Chair
Design Philip Arctander 1944
Paustian Furniture Collection

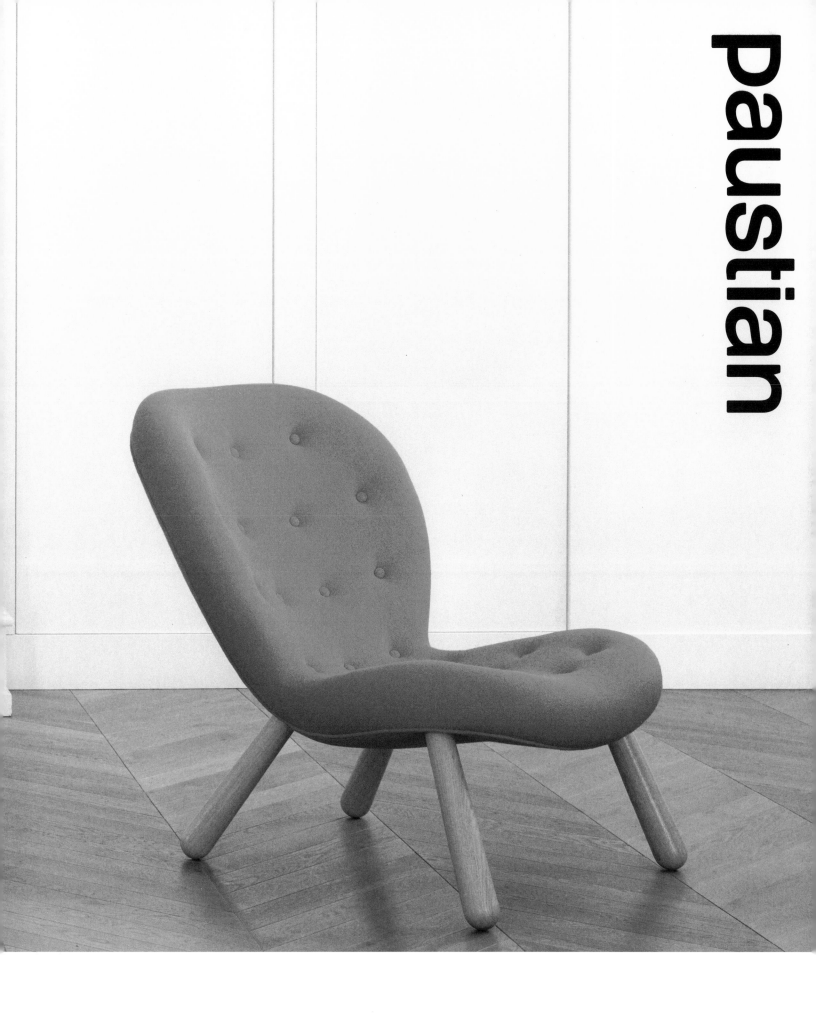

paustian

paustian.com

Frame: MYKITA LITE SUN KARLI | Photography: Mark Borthwick

HANDMADE IN BERLIN

BERLIN | CARTAGENA | COPENHAGEN | LOS ANGELES | MONTERREY | NEW YORK | PARIS | TOKYO | VIENNA | WASHINGTON | ZERMATT | ZURICH

SHOP ONLINE AT MYKITA.COM

The Naturalist:
Anita Calero

Words
Diana Budds

Photographs
Stefan Heinrichs

Styling
Alpha Vomero

"Coming back to Colombia is what I needed. I missed my roots, my soil, my birds, my smells, my fruit, my surroundings—my world that I left not loving."

During her years as a prop stylist and photographer in New York, Anita Calero honed a knack for spotting perfection in the imperfect and discerning elegance in the everyday. Whether it was in the outfits she constructed to go dancing at Studio 54 or in the shoots she did for some of the biggest magazines of the '80s, Anita pushed the boundaries of her own creativity. Now, after four decades, she is following the call back home to her native Colombia.

In order to capture life in photographs, you need to have lived it first. From making ends meet chauffeuring Greek royalty in a gold Cadillac during her younger years to shooting some of the world's biggest brands in her later decades, photographer and stylist Anita Calero has certainly made her time count. Though she is best known for capturing sublime still lifes, her reputation as an artist is often preceded by her presence as a woman—she exudes effervescence and graciousness, and she possesses an invigorating aura that belies her years. At 63, Anita is now embarking on the next chapter of her personal narrative: a homecoming of sorts to her native Cali, Colombia.

After almost four decades spent living and working in New York, Anita recently sold nearly all her possessions and decamped from the frenetic city to a simpler place where her family takes priority. "I had friends, colleagues and great art directors in New York, but family was missing," she says. "I think my life was meant to end up in Colombia." Though a brief flirtation with retirement ignited the shift in her mind-set, this move is less about grinding to a screeching halt and more about adopting balance.

During her years in America, Anita became known for her prop styling and photography work, which runs the gamut from interiors to food spreads and product shoots. "I don't like monotony," she says. "In the studio, outside of the studio, I like the variety." Regardless of her client or subject matter, Anita makes what's opposite her lens truly shine: A freshly butchered pork chop looks as sumptuous as an Italian leather handbag; a sweatshirt from UNIQLO as exalted as linens from Missoni. "I want to bring the beauty out of the mundane," she says. "I always compose scenes to give objects a life of their own."

Anita's knack for coaxing elegance from the everyday started at an early age. The second youngest of six children, she grew up in a creative household and found solace on her family's farm in Colombia amid the vast fields, open skies and spirited horses. This stoked her love of the natural world—a through-line in her life. "I was always enamored with nature," she says. "I'd climb trees and stay out there for hours. I was fascinated with the wind and the way trees moved." Her father, an MIT-educated civil engineer, had a business importing motors, which often arrived in wood crates. Instead of throwing them out, her mother saw potential in the wood and saved them to build custom furniture for the house. Her parents' resourcefulness and ability to perceive something beyond its prescribed value came to inform how Anita herself viewed the world: that the right eye can elicit beauty in the unexpected.

During her teenage years, Anita went through a freewheeling streak—one that arguably continued into her adult life. She never hewed to the rigid structure of a classroom, preferring and yearning for more freedom instead. "I wasn't a good student, meaning I had a lot of art in me," she quips. After she received a few failing grades, Anita's parents decided to send her abroad. At 15 she embarked on a two-year stint in Switzerland to learn French ("Switzerland taught me organization, which I love," she says. "It goes with my Virgo personality"), then she went on to live in England for a year. Coming of age in Europe during the '60s and '70s exposed her to a range of cultural experiences that she might not have encountered otherwise. "I wouldn't say that I was rebellious; I was curious," she says. "I was both a hippie and a

KINFOLK.COM, REFRESHED

Find more people, design, travel and culture
every day on our new site, launching mid-November.

KINFOLK

EDITOR-IN-CHIEF
Nathan Williams

EDITOR
Julie Cirelli

CREATIVE DIRECTOR
Anja Charbonneau

DEPUTY EDITOR
John Clifford Burns

DESIGN DIRECTOR
Alex Hunting

ASSISTANT EDITOR
Molly Mandell

COPY EDITOR
Rachel Holzman

PROOFREADER
Kelsey Burrow

WEB ADMINISTRATOR
Jesse Hiestand

COMMUNICATIONS DIRECTOR
Jessica Gray

ADVERTISING DIRECTOR
Pamela Mullinger

PUBLISHING DIRECTOR
Amy Woodroffe

SALES & DISTRIBUTION DIRECTOR
Frédéric Mähl

ACCOUNTING MANAGER
Paige Bischoff

OUUR DESIGNER
Mario Depicolzuane

MANAGING DIRECTOR
Doug Bischoff

STUDIO MANAGER
Monique Schröder

EDITORIAL ASSISTANTS
Lucrezia Biasutti
Ulrika Lukševica

DESIGN ASSISTANTS
Eleanor Bok Lund
Daniel Norman
Benja Pavlin

OPERATIONS ASSISTANT
Margriet Kalsbeek

CONTRIBUTING EDITORS
Michael Anastassiades
Jonas Bjerre-Poulsen
Ilse Crawford
Frida Escobedo
Leonard Koren
Hans Ulrich Obrist
Amy Sall
Matt Willey

ILLUSTRATION
Chidy Wayne

STYLING & SET DESIGN
Maya Angeli
Atelier CPH
Eden Dawn
Natasha Felker
Ilona Hamer
Aliki Kirmitsi
Martin Persson
Carolyne Rapp
My Ringsted
Sandy Suffield
Alpha Vomero
Emily Whitmore

WORDS
Alex Anderson
Alice Cavanagh
Danielle Demetriou
Erin Dixon
Madeleine Dore
Rachel Gallaher
Molly Rose Kaufman
Jared Killeen
Harriet Fitch Little
Sarah Moroz
Micah Nathan
Tristan Rutherford
Charles Shafaieh
Suzanne Snider
Trey Taylor
Pip Usher
Molly Young

PHOTOGRAPHY
Holly Andres
Sarah Bunter
Mirjam Bleeker
Lasse Fløde
Terry deRoy Gruber
Denise Grünstein
Guido Harari
Marsý Hild Þórsdóttir
Andreas Larsson
Delfino Legnani
Noel Manalili
Boe Marion
Rory van Millingen
Christopher Morris
Mikkel Mortensen
Hasse Nielsen
Edward Quinn
Anders Schønnemann
Charlie Schuck
Aaron Tilley
Zoltan Tombor

PUBLICATION DESIGN
Alex Hunting

ISSUE 22

info@kinfolk.com
www.kinfolk.com

Published by Ouur Media
Amagertorv 14, Level 1
1160 Copenhagen, Denmark

The views expressed in Kinfolk magazine are those of the respective contributors and are not necessarily shared by the company or its staff.

SUBSCRIBE
Kinfolk is published four times a year. To subscribe, visit www.kinfolk.com/subscribe or email us at subscribe@kinfolk.com

CONTACT US
If you have questions or comments, please write to us at info@kinfolk.com. For advertising inquiries, get in touch at advertising@kinfolk.com

Printed in Canada
by Hemlock Printers Ltd.

@LEVISMADEANDCRAFTED

ARTFUL CONSTRUCTION. ELEVATED DETAILS.
LEVI'S® BY DESIGN.

"If you invest too much into your competitiveness, you lose perspective."
SOPHIE HICKS — P.148

Photograph: Anders Schønnemann

ERIK
Jørgensen
THE MANUFACTURER

QUALITY AS A TOP PRIORITY

Erik Jørgensen was founded in 1954 in Svendborg, Denmark, by saddlemaker and upholsterer Erik Jørgensen. Erik Jørgensen's collection consists of well-known classics from Hans J. Wegner and Poul M. Volther as well as new furniture produced in collaboration with new young designers.

At Erik Jørgensen we aim to produce furniture that lasts. Not only for use but also to beautify our surroundings, and open our eyes to new ways of seeing and making furniture. A passion for design and good craftsmanship is what characterizes Erik Jørgensen.

WWW.ERIK-JOERGENSEN.COM

PART THREE

Work

"You would never write on a person's face, so you should never write on their business card."

TIPS — P.166

Photograph: Zoltan Tombor, Stylist: Alpha Vomero

Rich
Brilliant
Willing

Contemporary LED lighting designed and manufactured in New York.

T +1 212 388 1621   www.RichBrilliantWilling.com   Born in Brooklyn

Welcome

Success is often presented as a fixed destination, after which life should coast smoothly along. In reality, "success" is a mere starting point, a leveling up after which unknown and unknowable challenges await. Many have sought a magic formula for professional success, particularly when it comes to creative or innovative work.

In 1990, cognitive biologist John Hayes published a paper that would provide a working blueprint for several generations of creative entrepreneurs. Surveying a group of students at Carnegie Mellon University, he discovered that successful creative work was dependent on four personal characteristics: devotion to the task (the kind of "devotion" that falls somewhere between a healthy work ethic and what Hayes quotes as "absorption in work, over long years, and frequently to the exclusion of everything else"); the ability to work independently without falling prey to "fashions" or conventions; the quest for originality; and, perhaps most importantly, flexibility in the face of difficulty or hardship.

In other words, do the work. Put in the time. Master your craft. And don't panic over professional failures—they're a natural part of the work process.

This sentiment is echoed again and again within this issue of *Kinfolk*, wherein we feature a special section devoted to work. Flexibility—the ability to roll with the punches, to separate the public-facing side of our personalities from our private identities—is just as important as raw talent, if not more so. This might mean equipping ourselves with the ability to work under pressure or to deal with disappointment, like Stine Goya, who after 10 years at the helm of her fashion label, has come to expect a certain percentage of failure from each project.

In our regular features section, Swedish perfumer Ben Gorham translates some of the most difficult experiences of his personal life into the evocative scents produced by his company, Byredo. In the *Brief History of Personality Tests* on page 62, Harriet Fitch Little traces the dubious history of personality tests like Myers-Briggs, which claim to tell us who we are based on whether we prefer the center of the room or the wall at a party. Elsewhere, in our roundtable discussion on page 132, a clinical psychologist and a life coach explain the healthy and not-so-healthy dynamics that arise within groups.

Lastly, we present Hans Ulrich Obrist, one of our new contributing editors. Each issue, *Kinfolk* invites industry leaders to offer expert insider perspectives on the fields of design, food and fashion. On page 189, Obrist—a permanent fixture on the exhibition circuit and an integral member of Kinfolk's new editorial board—answers a few rapid-fire questions and leaves us with some required reading recommendations, from Etel Adnan to Édouard Glissant.

If this issue looks and feels new, it's because we've redesigned the magazine to create a more dynamic reading experience. Keeping what's essential to *Kinfolk*—our core values and considered approach to life—we've expanded the magazine to include more voices and special sections, and to delve deeper into the things we love most: examining the lives we live, why and how we live them, and doing so with intention, energy and a sense of community.

NATHAN WILLIAMS & JULIE CIRELLI

MORTON & MABEL

1

Starters

ALEX ANDERSON

The Art of Conversation

Beyond small talk and silence: How to cultivate good conversation.

Whether great conversation traverses easy or difficult terrain, its reward is a more poignant connection with others. But to converse well is challenging. The art of conversation lacks well-defined rules, yet places high demands on our capabilities. Perhaps it is helpful to consider philosopher Michael Oakeshott's brilliantly concise description of conversation as "unrehearsed intellectual adventure." In these three quick words he beautifully encapsulates the spontaneity, challenge and pleasure of this quintessentially human social interplay.

To say that conversation is unrehearsed is to acknowledge that it depends on the moment. It thrives not on plans or goals but on improvisation. (Dialogue with the hope of some gain is not conversation; it is lecture, competition or interview.) There is an unspoken consensus among linguists that conversation is process-oriented, that its course cannot be predetermined. University of California, Berkeley philosopher John Searle once lamented that "conversation does not have an intrinsic structure about which a relevant theory can be formulated." Vexingly to those who prefer tidy models for human interaction, in conversation there can be no strict rules.

Nevertheless, skilled conversationalists keep things on track by observing some basic guidelines. First, listening and speaking are both key because, as Searle writes, conversation "must be seen as an expression of shared intentionality." Second, remaining good-natured and flexible is crucial. Benjamin Franklin contends that "complaisance" and "agreeableness" facilitate good conversation. "Complaisance," Franklin explains, "is a seeming preference of others to ourselves," and "agreeableness" is "a readiness to overlook or excuse their foibles."

This suggests a third guideline: to converse with a good sense of humor, which is why David Hume, the great philosopher of human nature, prizes "wit and ingenuity" above all in conversation. So, the rules, such as they are, come down to listening well and activating sociable traits of courtesy, goodwill and humor. All of these require attunement not just to the themes that arise, but also to others in the conversation. Poet and novelist Ursula K. Le Guin calls this attention to each other "mutual phase locking" or "entrainment." "We need to talk together," she says, "speaker and hearer here, now." Good conversation may be unrehearsed, but it isn't haphazard; it is careful, balanced and generous.

Proposing that conversation should be intellectual is not to demand only deep insights or high-minded discourse. Rather, it insists on thoughtfulness. Even small talk can turn to good conversation if intelligently undertaken. Observations about food, clothes, weather or sports easily lead to consequential matters among well-informed, inventive conversationalists. When conversation turns to weighty issues, familiarity with facts and subtleties makes a difference, while agreeableness and good humor keep things moving along.

These ensure that even difficult discussions—of politics or religion, for instance—don't bog down in bias and anger. Thoughtful attention to others in the conversation can also help keep it from becoming antagonistic. In an era when etiquette may have fallen out of favor, it is still worth listening to etiquette authority Emily Post, who declares, "nearly all the faults or mistakes in conversation are caused by not thinking." Thinking people who don't agree can still connect. This is partly because intelligence in conversation is not solely cerebral. When Ursula K. Le Guin talks about entrainment in conversation, she describes it not just as a meeting of minds but a physical resonance among bodies. Because conversation involves listening, speech and expression (posture, hand gestures, subtle facial movements), the whole biological apparatus comes into play. When we say that we are "deep in conversation" we acknowledge this comprehensive, resonant connection.

Connection becomes especially important if we think about conversation as an adventure. When talk moves to unanticipated places, everyone involved has to contribute as equals. Deference may be appropriate in greetings, but conversation cruises on the assumption of equivalence. This can be challenging in situations of perceived imbalance—a professor talking casually with a student, meeting a fiancée's parents, breaking in with a group who know each other well. To navigate these requires thoughtful attunement to the experience and understanding of others. Spontaneous, intelligent conversation among equals opens passages to new knowledge, understanding and insight; it doesn't merely follow one person's lead or traverse well-trodden paths. Instead, listening well, thinking generously and speaking with good humor and ingenuity are the best equipment for participating in great conversation.

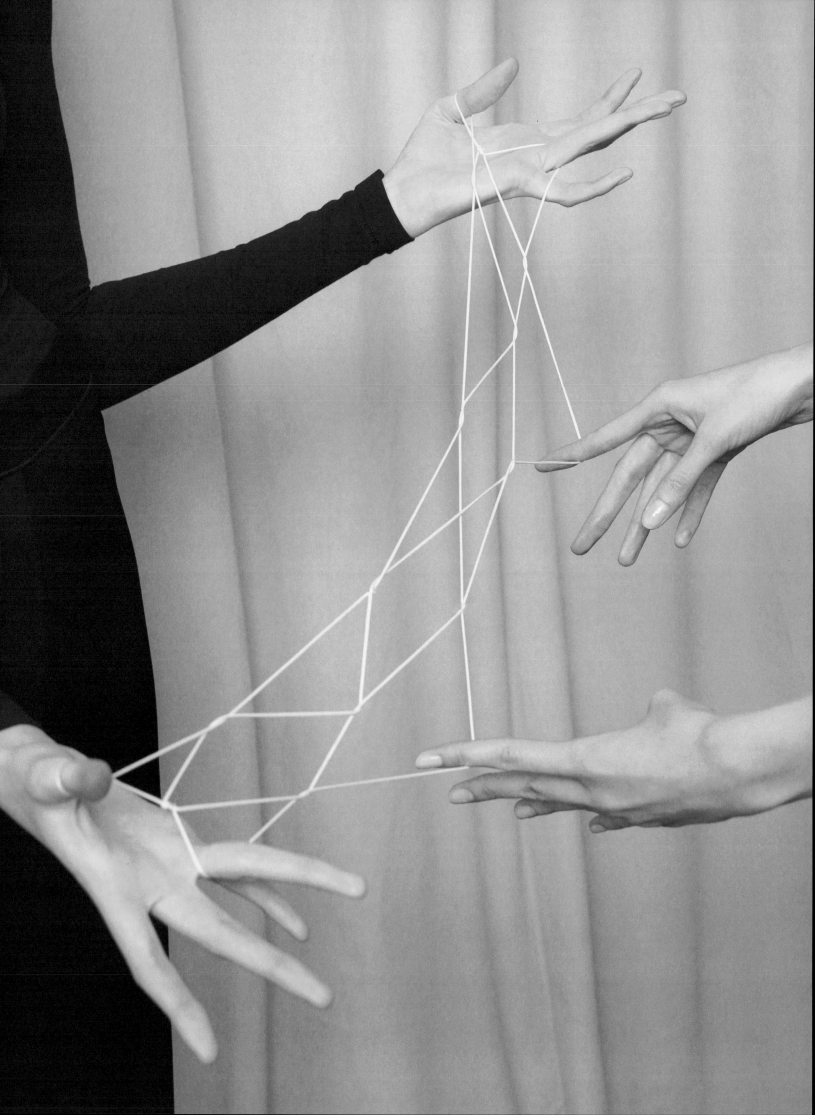

AS TOLD TO ALICE CAVANAGH
Pauline Deltour

Paris-based designer *Pauline Deltour* isn't afraid to walk the razor-sharp line between art and design.

"When I was young, I wasn't very aware of objects. Today, I'm so sensitive to them that I only keep a few of my own objects at home. I would hate to feel invaded by my own designs, but I enjoy being surrounded by the work of others, like Eileen Gray, Pierre Charpin and Maarten van Severen. I'm also addicted to books, to the point where I rarely allow myself to visit design museums because I nearly always leave the shop with yet more books.

My office is in the 10th arrondissement in Paris—one of my favorite parts of the city. Like the seaside coast of Brittany where I grew up—where the wind and rain seem to leave their marks in the shapes of people's faces—Paris leaves a mark on its people. There's a certain rhythm in the French capital that's shaped from the speed with which we do things (even if we do complain a lot while we're doing them).

When it comes to my approach to design, I keep it simple: I strive to create useful objects, not to make decoration for the sake of it. Function is what distinguishes a designer from an artist. Awareness of the objects that surround us is not automatic; it develops only if you train your mind on it."

Left: Pauline has created designs for Lexon and Alessi, the latter of whom she met while working with Konstantin Grcic. Pauline wears a dress by Perret Schaad.

Photograph: Noel Manalili

Right photograph: Aaron Tilley, Set Design by Maya Angeli & Aliki Kirmitsi. Left photographs: Mikkel Mortensen, Prop styling: Atelier CPH

HOLE UP
by Molly Mandell

In a seemingly endless variety of shapes, sizes and patterns, holes add eye-catching elements to architecture and design while providing functionality by screening light, filtering sound, increasing weather resistance and improving energy efficiency. Pettersen & Hein's mirror sculpture (top) punctures ideas about art and design—literally and figuratively—by transforming everyday materials and objects into something more unexpected. The clock designed by Birgitte Due Madsen and Jonas Trampedach (center) features hexagonal patterns that allow even numbers to be easily identified. The holes in HAY's punched organizer (bottom) create a sense of uniformity and inspire tidier desks at the office and at home.

JOHN CLIFFORD BURNS

Word: Trypophobia

More commonly known as the fear of holes, trypophobia is a word with both its etymology and experience rooted in the recesses of the internet.

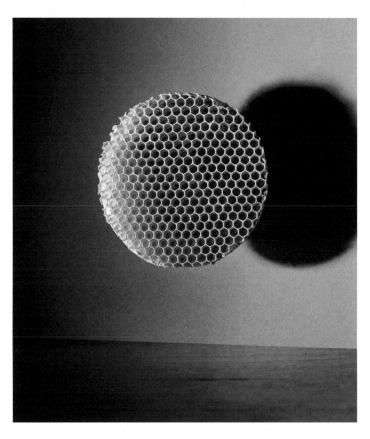

Etymology: From *trýpa* meaning "drilling holes" and *phobos* meaning "fear".

Meaning: As with other phobias, trypophobia refers to an irrational fear—in this case, an anxiety or revulsion induced by holes, bumps or pockmarks clustered together. Barnacles, sponges and aerated soap foam are known stimulants of trypophobia. Other triggers include skin lesions and cheese graters, which bring on symptoms such as dread, itchiness and hot sweat.

Perhaps, as voids in solid mass, holes seem spectral in their inherent implication that something is missing—unless one follows the reverse logic of American minimalist artist Carl Andre. He thought of sculpture not as cuts in materials but as cuts in space formed by materials: "A thing is a hole in a thing it is not," he once wrote. Arnold Wilkins and Geoff Cole, research psychologists at the University of Essex, UK, however, have put forward the idea that trypophobia is not actually triggered by holes, but by the brain's reaction to the repeated contrasts between light and dark detail within a given line of sight—a similar brain reaction to the markings characteristic of deadly animals.

Use: Germinating in the underbelly of internet forums, trypophobia began to surface in 2005 as a proposed term to describe the disgust prompted by honeycombs and other holey items. Offline, however, there remains skepticism surrounding its use; there are no recorded mentions of the term in medical literature and it is neither recognized nor used in the diagnostic manual of the American Psychological Association.

Trypophobia's primary use online as click bait suggests it has developed as a socially produced fear like tetraphobia, a fear of the number four that grips East Asia. After all, one is much less likely to wig out when seeing cheese graters or Swiss cheese offline and in the kitchen than online and accompanied by images of skin lesions.

CHARLES SHAFAIEH

The Shadow Self

Just as our bodies cast shadows on the ground, our conscious minds cast shadows over certain elements of our persona—the parts of ourselves that we choose to keep in the dark.

Photograph: Denise Grünstein / CameraLink

"Life is born only of the spark of opposites," wrote Carl Jung, the Swiss analytic psychologist. The two opposing forces that he referred to were the conscious mind and what he called "the shadow" —a collection of all-too-often repressed traits, the existence of which most of us deny. Its hazy and indistinct contours contain "all those unpleasant qualities we like to hide," from arrogance to greed, recklessness and illicit urges. And despite any efforts to the contrary, Jung proposed that this inner Caliban—one's Puckish side—cannot be silenced or bottled up. It will make itself known to each of us in myriad ways, whether as strange figures appearing in dreams or, most commonly, through projections of those denied traits and qualities onto others.

"Projections change the world into the replica of one's own unknown face," Jung wrote in his 1951 text, *Aion: Researches into the Phenomenology of the Self*. He went on to describe a solipsistic world consumed by self-made illusions. The more a person tries to hide or subvert the shadow self, the more power those impulses have over their consciousness—with painful consequences.

Sadegh Hedayat illustrates this dilemma in his hallucinogenic 1936 novel, *The Blind Owl*. "I am afraid to look out of the window of my room or to look at myself in the mirror for everywhere I see my own shadow multiplied indefinitely," states the narrator, immersed in a feverish dream. Filled with haunting images of a crime he may or may not have committed, the dream repeats itself in various iterations ad infinitum. The kaleidoscopic effect this cycle creates is dizzying. As Hedayat's prose demonstrates, when one's world closes in upon itself, all distinctions become meaningless: Guilt and innocence, fact and fiction, reason and madness all blur.

Perhaps most tragic is that denying the shadow severs our ability to form bonds with others, making empathy impossible. Poet Forough Farrokhzad entreats us to resist this isolationism in her sole film, *The House is Black* (1963). At the opening of this lyrical short documentary about life in a leper colony, a voice intones, "There is no shortage of ugliness in the world. If man closed his eyes to it, there would be even more." The leper colony—a community cast out by most societies—is an ideal metaphor for the shadow. Farrokhzad both makes us look and has our gaze returned. Yet she does not sentimentalize her subjects—neither their appearance nor their pain—making it indiscernible who, among those in the film or those watching, is healthy and who is scarred, and thus where this blackness begins and ends.

Coming to terms with one's shadow self is just the beginning of a lifelong undertaking that Jung called *individuation*, or the process in which the conscious part of one's personality begins acknowledging, and even listening to, the unconscious. This movement toward integration is reflected in the abstract sculptures of Anish Kapoor. Approached head-on, *Monochrome (Grey)* appears as a deep gray hole opening forever into an abyss. Moving just slightly left or right, however, reveals a white bowl that juts out over a foot from the wall—with only the interior painted. In Kapoor's words, "'Something' that dwells in the presence of the work... allows it or forces it not to be what it states it is in the first stance." As with his reflective stainless steel sculptures that often distort and even conceal the spectator's image, this piece elicits an anxious, provocative sensation upon revealing its true form. In an instant, surfaces turn corrupt; the safe, comfortable and knowable become untrustworthy.

Jung understood that seeing what lies hidden within us—like staring into Kapoor's void—causes confusion, even pain. But as writer Jun'ichiro Tanizaki reminds us, "Were it not for shadows, there would be no beauty."

A self-described introvert, rising architect *Bernard Dubois* is like his work—not as serious as he first appears.

AS TOLD TO MOLLY MANDELL

Bernard Dubois

Right: Detail from Bernard's interior for Valextra's flagship store in Milan, Italy.

Architect Bernard Dubois has been on the fast track since graduating from Brussels' École de La Cambre in 2009. In less than 10 years, he has opened his own studio, curated the Belgian Pavilion at Venice Architecture Biennale 2014 and designed retail projects for brands such as Nicolas Andreas Taralis and Valextra. As Bernard travels and works abroad—in France, Italy, Switzerland and China—more and more frequently, his appreciation for his Belgian roots only seems to grow.

———

"My biggest strength is also my biggest weakness: I'm a very systematic person. I don't believe in creative moments where you're touched by the grace of God and then suddenly have a great design in hand. Usually, those moments don't happen.

When I first visit a site or meet with a client, I try not to say too much. Instead, I listen and attempt to understand the environment. We start with many options and narrow them down. This creates a certain quality, in the end, because the project has really been thought through.

Sometimes a client expects me to think up something visionary immediately and might be disappointed when I don't come up with a concept on the spot. I need to process an environment and work through all of my ideas, and that can be very understated. I prefer to think about things. I'm a very quiet person on the outside, but I'm very loud on the inside. It's important not to mistake my external quietness as real quietness. In Belgian humor, it's normal to make fun of yourself. There's a quiet sense of self-mockery that's reflected in my work. The exterior might look serious, but it's not really as serious as it appears.

I'm also a photographer, so I photograph a lot of my own projects. When a project is complete and I go to take pictures, I'm always disappointed. The angles that I thought were the most interesting aren't, and I think, "This project is a failure." But usually, when I look back at the photographs, I find that there are angles that are much more interesting than what I had originally imagined to be the best.

In the end, when a project is finally finished, it doesn't belong to the architect anymore. It belongs to the user and its environment. Everyone has a right to rediscover a space in their own way and to find their own particular angles and views."

Photograph: Delfino Legnani

AGJEANS.COM

TREY TAYLOR

Cult Rooms: Picasso

Pablo Picasso worked in seven different studios through his life. In one—a converted parfumerie—he painted war with peace, and a little quiet.

In 1948, Pablo Picasso moved to the south of France. As a staunch communist and cherished member of the French Communist Party, he had been invited to the town of Vallauris by the local party administration to paint the nave of a Cistercian chapel.

An advocate for peace, Picasso had hoped to create a work that depicted a fight "against war." He ended up producing *La Guerre et La Paix*—one of his largest murals. Pieced together from an exhaustive 300 preparatory sketches, the work was inspired by his rereading of Leo Tolstoy's epic novel, *War and Peace*.

Picasso became consumed by the project, his idea becoming larger than anything the modest villa he shared with his mistress, Françoise Gilot, could house.

So he moved into a former parfumerie, Le Fournas, readying himself for a battle of his own by constructing a three-level wooden structure replete with an interior staircase that the poet Claude Roy would later describe as looking like a Roman assault tower.

Picasso confided in Roy, describing his mark on the chapel: "If peace wins in the world, the war I have painted will be a thing of the past... The only blood that flows will be before a fine drawing, a beautiful picture. People will get too close to it, and when they scratch it a drop of blood will form, showing that the work is truly alive."

For Picasso, Le Fournas was not just a new atelier but a deeply personal and private space. Following lunch with Picasso in September 1952, his friend Jean Cocteau—the multihyphenate French artist and poet—wrote in his diary that, "From two in the afternoon until 10 at night, Picasso locks himself in with his fresco. Nobody is admitted. Not even Françoise."

Left: Le Fournas was Picasso's private refuge and the site of some of his most iconic works, including the towering mural *La Guerre et La Paix*.

MICAH NATHAN

On Procrastination

If good things come to those who wait, what happens to those who keep others waiting? A slightly overdue defense of procrastination.

The irony of this essay is implicit in its subject: Not only did I procrastinate before writing it, but everyone reading this essay—with the exception of my editor—is procrastinating by reading it. There is something better you should be doing. By something "better" I mean something utilitarian: paying bills, finishing homework, cleaning dirty windows, getting a colonoscopy, etc. From this claim arises several assumptions:

First, we only procrastinate that which is both painful and necessary; we wouldn't procrastinate throwing ourselves on a hot spike because we would never do so. Unless hot-spiking was for pleasurable ends, in which case we wouldn't procrastinate.

Second, what is necessary is often painful: paying bills, finish-

Photograph: Aaron Tilley, Set Design by Maya Angeli & Aliki Kirmitsi

ing homework, cleaning dirty windows, getting a colonoscopy, etc.

Third, doing painful, necessary things as soon as possible, i.e., pre-crastination, is more virtuous than procrastinating.

These assumptions are self-evident; I only listed them for emphasis. The war against procrastination is as familiar as the war on death: both are constant and futile. Mary Todd Lincoln referred to procrastination as her "evil genius." Benjamin Franklin—always good for laconic truths spiced with the occasional wink-wink—said, "You may delay, but time will not." Pablo Picasso warned, in his usual understated manner, "Only put off until tomorrow what you are willing to die having left undone." I agree with all of them. I agree but I don't care to stop pro-

crastinating because I enjoy procrastinating. I don't care about the studies measuring how miserable or happy test subjects claim to be when waiting to perform difficult tasks versus starting those difficult tasks, and I don't care about the fines accrued by filing taxes late or the 401(k) contributions missed due to delaying retirement planning, because people ultimately do what they want (assuming they're fortunate enough to live a mostly autonomous life), and if a financial and/or existential penalty is the price of putting off uncomfortable necessities, then it's a price set by the consumer. Blaming procrastination for the things that don't get done is like blaming overeating for obesity; it's general enough to be true but too easy an explanation. Procrastination is the

symptom, not the disease. The story goes that someone asked Hemingway what the best method was for writing a novel. A stupid question deserving of a lethal answer, and Hemingway didn't disappoint.

"First you defrost the refrigerator," he supposedly replied. Of course defrosting refrigerators has nothing to do with novel-writing but we know what he meant. The painful (for everyone), necessary (for writers, at least) task of writing a novel requires procrastination. We procrastinate until we're ready, and if we're never ready, well, we were never going to write that novel anyway.

One argument against this essay is the Calvinistic response: *Procrastination is a sign of weakness and indicates a lack of discipline.* This brings us back to the third as-

sumption, that pre-crastination is a virtue, that doing what is painful and necessary as soon as possible demonstrates character. My Paganic response: Attaching morality to time-management is the equivalent of a perfect attendance award, a consolation prize given to self-righteous prigs who believe the universe keeps score. Fruit falls when it's ripe, truth is confirmed by inspection and delay, there are no honors too distant to the man who prepares himself for them with patience—in other words, we'll get to it when we're ready.

In other words, if we procrastinate our colonoscopy and we get colon cancer, it might be tragic and it might be selfish, but it was our decision. You can't complain about the bill when you sent it to yourself.

MADELEINE DORE

Christopher Esber

Sharpen one skill set for slow-burning success: How a Sydney-based designer does business.

Photograph: Christopher Morris; Styling: Ilona Hamer

At a young age, Australian designer Christopher Esber was given a crucial piece of advice: Put all of your energy into one thing and learn to do it very well. He's shaped his approach to life and work around this notion. In time, it has earned him an international reputation for his exploratory design and precision tailoring. Yet perhaps more importantly, doing one thing well has served as an antidote to the designer's greatest fear—mediocrity. Instead of being paralyzed by the enormity of his grand ideas, or abandoning his plans or passions when the going got rough, Esber has used his fear of mediocrity as fuel both for his imagination and his ambition.

Has your work process changed over time? There's something quite naive about how I create collections. I first sat behind a sewing machine when I was eight years old. I was just making it up as I went along. There was no strict idea of how a shirt should be made and that freedom has impacted how I do things now.

I don't really abide by the fundamentals. Of course, they are there, especially from a construction and tailoring point of view, but when conceptualizing with the team it's quite open and experimental. We can take a trench element and put it on a skirt and that

seems completely normal. An idea might not work out, but sometimes it does and that is so exciting.

Is there a secret to discovering your strengths? You need to be open to exploring and trying new things. It can be difficult because you might discover you're good at something, but not necessarily enjoy it. I was lucky in that from an early age, I always knew what I wanted to do and could put all my energy into building on my knowledge of tailoring. With knowledge comes power and greater scope in terms of how things can be twisted and reimagined.

How has a fear of mediocrity shaped your approach to work? A fear of mediocrity is my biggest motivator and it informs everything I do—not in some terrorizing way, but as a daily ambition. It can be a powerful driving force to always question what you're doing and why and really push yourself. After all, who wants to be mediocre? Who wants to look back and think, "Well, that was fine, I guess."

How much attention do you pay to trends? I try to stay away from what's on trend because it can be so monotonous. Of course, it's good to be aware of what's happening in the fashion landscape, but whenever I'm designing a collec-

tion I try not to look at anything else—even social media. There's so much superfluous information that gets stored in your brain and you really have to distance yourself. You need to become immersed in your own world and rethink what you want to see in a particular garment.

Do you find it difficult to switch off? I'm finally at the stage now where I can have a weekend. Early on in my career, my work was all-consuming, but I've come to realize that you gain the most clarity when you have time away. Even just going for a walk, a solution will come to you that never would have if you fixated on the work. Switching off provides more clarity in terms of an idea or the direction I want to take the brand.

Would you say that you have achieved success? I would describe my career as slow-burning—in that nothing has come easily for me. I didn't have any experience working for someone else and early on people would tell me to quit while I was ahead. I was quite alone and had to learn along the way, but I realized recently that I am where I once dreamed of being. You get so caught up with deadlines or focused on different milestones that you don't take the time to stop and reflect on how far you've come.

Right: Christopher wears a shirt by Burberry and a coat by Raf Simons.

MICAH NATHAN

International Klein Blue

Between 1957 and his death in 1962, artist *Yves Klein* painted just short of 200 works using only one color—his own.

International Klein Blue is one of the few colors you never forget seeing for the first time, like the red shock of fresh blood or the shine of chrome or the lurid pink of a post-thunderstorm sunset. IKB looks like it would set off a Geiger counter—a hot, glowing, Aegean blue that seems on the verge of reaching critical mass. It is a color patented by the French painter Yves Klein (1928-1962), the short-lived provocateur who dabbled in photography and sculpture and Duchamp-inspired frivolities, but who is known primarily —unfairly, capitalistically, pick your adverb—for his monochromatic canvases saturated in IKB.

Klein's Nouveau Réalisme movement claimed to "appropriate" reality by expanding the definition of portraiture. Theirs was a representation of the world in formless hue and assemblage, not so much an interpretation as a distillation. What was the distillate? The color blue. Blue, according to Klein, "has no dimensions; it is beyond dimensions, whereas the other colors are not." Or something like that—the *why* in art is always less interesting than the *how* and neither are as interesting as the *what*. Klein's IKB contains a perfect blend of solvent and resin encapsulating pure ultramarine blue pigment, with each grain of pigment fossilized in a polyvinyl acetate resin before applying it—either by lambskin roller or from the nude bodies of models as in Klein's interesting-but-silly *Anthropometries of the Blue Epoch*— to a casein-coated canvas. In simpler terms: IKB is as much an ideal binding agent as it is a pigment.

The mechanic behind this Goldilocksean balance was Edouard Adam, a third-generation *marchand de couleurs* commissioned by Klein in 1956 to capture the essence of that pure ultramarine blue. Previous applications of the pigment were disappointing (once dry, the color turned insipid) so Adam experimented with a map waterproofing agent named Rhodopas M60A, added a dash of ethyl acetate, a pinch of ethyl alcohol and Klein's favorite color. Thus was born International Klein Blue, Soleau envelope no. 63471, registered in Paris on May 19, 1960.

When seen in its original state on a Klein canvas, IKB's effect startles: There's an uncanny depth, velvety without the nap, substantial yet delicate, and so radiant it seems as though Klein is still waiting for it to dry, perhaps sitting in the next room with his coven of nude models. This preserved freshness is Yves Klein's final provocation; the metaphor writes itself.

———

The Tate Liverpool's Yves Klein exhibit runs through March 5, 2017.

BLUE VELVET
by Molly Mandell

Color is subjective: What causes delight for one person might provoke hostility in another, which is why color can be the deciding factor in whether or not an item belongs in one's home. More than 50 years after its creation, Yves Klein's shade of blue still provides inspiration for designers. Some may be apprehensive about using a hue so closely connected to an artist as celebrated as Yves Klein, but those featured above show no fear. Toke Design's geometric side table (top) employs rich International Klein Blue to add vibrancy to the living room. The sculpture (center) and papercut (bottom), both by Leise Dich Abrahamsen, bring the deep blue hue back to the artist's studio and, someday, to the collector's home.

Photographs: Mikkel Mortensen, Prop styling: Atelier CPH

The co-founder of design firm *Overgaard & Dyrman* has discovered that it's one thing to be a leader in your field, quite another to be the leader of your team.

AS TOLD TO JOHN CLIFFORD BURNS

Jasper Overgaard

Left: She wears a coat by Maison Margiela from Luisaviaroma.
Right: Jasper wears a T-shirt by Won Hundred and jeans by Acne Studios.

Photograph: Hasse Nielsen, Styling: My Ringsted

"Christian Dyrman and I started as designers who had dreams of making furniture and focusing on craftsmanship. Then we found out that if our designs were to be as good as we wanted them to be, we had to hire people and teach them how to manufacture. All of a sudden, we were leaders.

We hadn't thought about that when we started out. Christian and I really love to stand there and make our own furniture, to dig deep into the small details ourselves. But the problem with doing that is that you're not able to develop a company. I think that's perhaps the biggest challenge for many small businesses: It's difficult to delegate.

From the day we quit our jobs, we focused 100 percent on our company. When you do that, you wear a lot of hats. In the beginning, for example, we were also the sales department and we weren't especially good at that. That's not the way it should be: We should really be focusing on what we are good at—designing and developing.

We want staff that share our ideas and mentality; we really want to bond. But that can also be a problem in itself. For example, if we're hiring a metal worker who is extremely good at welding, then it shouldn't matter what they think about the world or the small things.

But I like to be close to the people that I work with; I often focus on being a good friend. My concern now—as a leader—is to not focus so much on my own personal relationships but on the relationships and collaborations between my employees.

Leadership is becoming a challenge that I really like: I see it as a design task in itself. It can be basic: How is the light in the factory? Is there enough fresh air? How does a worker feel at the workstation? Then, how do they feel about their work? How is the relationship between this person and the one next to them? Do they work well together? And when they take a break, do they feel comfortable with each other? In the end, that's the right person for us.

My responsibility is, in many ways, finding out how to put all of these bricks together and making it work as well as it can. If I think of it as leading a company, it's a very tough task, but if I think of it as design it makes things much more interesting."

BOLD MOVES

by Jared Killeen

Marcel Duchamp made artwork, but he also played chess. So ardently did he pursue the latter—joining a prestigious chess club in Paris, competing in national tournaments—that his admirers might wonder whether he was truly happy as an artist. It seems Duchamp asked himself the same question. In 1920, after threatening to abandon the art world and study chess full time, he wrote, "Naturally this is the part of my life that I enjoy most." His love of chess is evident in his work: The figures in *The Large Glass* recall rooks arranged carefully on a board. Duchamp wished to fuse art and chess. The popular opinion, espoused by historians, proposes that Duchamp saw the art world as a game, his opponent the entire history of Western aesthetics. (According to this theory, his infamous readymades were the equivalent of a checkmate.) But anyone who's played chess knows there is a difference between a game, where one player attempts to outdo the other, and a problem, which requires one to develop a scenario for another to solve. Thus, it's more accurate to say that Duchamp wished to compose problems for his audience— problems of aesthetics and philosophy, resolved only through contemplation. In this way, he invites us to play with him, even in his absence. *Photograph by Aaron Tilley & Set Design by Maya Angeli & Aliki Kirmitsi*

ERIN DIXON

Esperanza Spalding

More than two and a half decades into a musical career that began at the age of five, *Esperanza Spalding* continues to challenge expectations and classifications—particularly her own.

Esperanza Spalding's signature instrument is the timeless and unaffected bass—an apt emblem for an artist whose concept of engagement centers less on the zeitgeist of social media and more on considered conversations and uninhibited creative expression. Since winning a Grammy for Best New Artist in 2011, Spalding has evolved this dialogue to incorporate acting, staging and directing, which, together, extend beyond entertainment to stir our collective capacity for constructive change.

How has music's place in your life changed over the years? I don't feel anymore that music is this thing that I have to practice and be good at so that people can tell I'm good, so that I can play with better musicians and continue to "advance" and grow and improvise and blah. This is life. This is my life. This gig is the world that I want. These musicians—the way we communicate with each other, the way we play with each other— we are practicing life. So it doesn't matter if it's music or it's acting or it's painting anymore. I'm looking for the same thing in my day-to-day life as any person who wants to grow more communicative and compassionate and connective.

Why are collaborations important as a musician? I'm putting myself in positions where I have to collaborate so that I can discover more about the true collaborative process. I've never really done that before—it kind of freaks me out and I'm not very good at it. That's the next frontier.

How has being a woman informed your path? Sometimes, I've been aware of interest in my work solely based on the novelty of me being a woman: Someone asks me to play because they want to hit on me or because they think having a girl playing will make their band look more appealing. Other times, I've experienced being invisible—what I'm actually doing, what I'm actually singing does not register with the listener because they aren't able to process me as a woman doing what I'm doing. Both of these things compel me to make sure that what I'm doing can stand on its own—if it were made by a man, or by anybody else.

What is music's role today, given the state of the world? It's like good-tasting food. No matter how bad it is out there, delicious food does more than just nourish you. If someone makes me the perfect scrambled eggs and the perfect bacon and the toast is thick, doughy, chewy, perfectly toasted, with the right kind of salty butter, I receive that. And as I'm being nourished, other things are activated from my center and emanate out into my body. I'm charged with a kind of well-being, a kind of joy or bliss that connects me with that person.

When I receive someone's creative expression that was made with love and care and intention, like those simple eggs, I get filled with inspiration and my gratitude gets activated and it changes the way that I interact with whatever happens next in my life. I'm liable to want to make it more beautiful and want to unpack the potential in it. Art, music, dance, film—whatever—all have this power to activate our own willingness to create more and reach for more and want to make whatever we're creating in the world beautiful and delicious. That fundamental desire is really important for social change. You have to feel compelled to adjust your actions to the well-being of others.

What is an important life lesson you've learned through your musical practice? Prepare, prepare, prepare. Let go.

Right: Esperanza's albums have earned her four Grammy Awards, including Best New Artist in 2011 and Best Jazz Vocal Album in 2013.

Photograph: Holly Andres, Styling: Eden Dawn

GEYSIR

REYKJAVÍK – HAUKADALUR – AKUREYRI

– geysir.com –

Still standing: design historian *Witold Rybczynski*'s appreciation of the chair and its 5,000-year history.

Photograph: Charlie Schuck, Set Design: Natasha Felker

JULIE CIRELLI

Origin of the Chair

Right: The carpeted Ring Chair by New York-based design studio Bower was designed by Danny Giannella and Tammer Hijazi in 2016.

In his latest book, *Now I Sit Me Down*, architect and writer Witold Rybczynski explores the history of the chair as an allegory of human evolution. "The astonishing historical variety of chairs is as much due to our intimate relationship with them as to functional imperatives," Rybczynski writes. By focusing so intensely on one thing—an exceedingly common object, the chair—Rybczynski charts a complex history driven as much by aesthetic caprice as tradition, craftsmanship and the immutable needs of the body.

History is littered with examples of furniture that were neither beautiful nor functional, but which advanced the development of design in some meaningful way. Like any genealogy, the chair's is rife with parallel strains, stubs, objects of dubious origin, mythologies and strange connections. The S-shaped curvature of a chair's splat, for example, which was first used in 10th-century China arrived in England around the 18th century.

The historical development of chair design has hardly followed a straight course. Ugly, impractical chairs are common in every stage of design development. "For instance, in seeking to reinvent the chair, designers of the Bauhaus ignored the history of design, creating chairs with flat seats and backs, and ignoring upholstery in favor of cushions," says Rybczynski. "The result was terribly uncomfortable." What, then, constitutes a perfect chair? Rybczynski believes that it's a marriage of form and function, like in the classic Arne Jacobsen *Series* 7 chair, an "excellent specimen" which, unlike Jacobsen's beloved but treacherous three-legged *Ant* chair, "does not have problems with stability, is very light, and supports you very nicely."

The Danish Modern movement combined traditional handicraft and materials into a new vernacular friendly both to the eye and the body. Yet for all their design acuity, the modernists weren't infallible. "Mies van der Rohe's *Barcelona* chair, while beautiful to look at, was a failure. It's difficult to get in and out of, and the back is too concave to be supportive."

The constraints of chair design —which Rybczynski defines as artistry, status, gravity, construction and comfort—keep it from straying too far from its essence as a place to sit. Rybczynski quotes George Kubler's classic *The Shape of Time*: "Everything made now is either a replica or a variant of something made a little time ago and so on back without break to the first morning of human time."

JOHN CLIFFORD BURNS

Theresa Traore Dahlberg

When *Theresa Traore Dahlberg* realized that she couldn't relate to narratives about women in West African films, she decided to make her own.

Theresa Traore Dahlberg is currently editing her first feature-length documentary, *Du Courage*, a bildungsroman shot in Burkina Faso. Her whole life, Theresa has split her time between the Sahelian nation and Sweden. It's an arrangement she says has broadened her perspective and instilled a versatility at her core—a valuable set of attributes for a documentary filmmaker. Knee-deep in more than 170 hours of footage, Theresa discusses her drive to persist, challenge stereotypes and deliver the West Africa she loves to a bigger screen and audience.

What are your working days currently like? I'm finishing my first feature documentary that was filmed in an all-girls school for car mechanics in Burkina Faso. It's a film about making choices, friendship, lost mothers and pretty much the everyday life of a teenage girl—a coming-of-age story in Ouagadougou. I'm also in my last year of studying fine arts at the Royal Academy of Fine Arts in Stockholm where I'm working on painting, sculpture and installation projects.

How do you decide what to document in your films? It completely depends on the project I'm working on. I decided that I wanted to do my last film, *Taxi Sister*, after

being in film school and having not seen even one inspiring film from the continent of Africa. Every time I saw an African film at school, I walked out feeling half as tall. The subjects were always war, poverty and disease. Of course, these stories should be told but if that's the only thing that you see then there's no balance. I felt like inspiring stories of women in West Africa were lacking. I also wanted to see more everyday stories that I could relate to. In general, what makes me want to document something is when I'm moved by a person or a place or if I'm passionate about a particular subject. It always starts with an initial gut feeling.

You spent a lot of time in West Africa yourself as a girl. I grew up in between Ouagadougou and the island of Öland in the southeastern part of Sweden. It's actually called the "Swedish savannah." I grew up there and I also grew up in Burkina Faso—back and forth.

How do you think that's shaped you? First of all, it gave me language. I've always spoken French, Swedish and English. It definitely gave me a wider perspective and also flexibility—the ability to adapt and pretty much feel at home in a new place. It was very important for my parents that we

played with kids from different backgrounds from a young age. For me, the understanding that people are the same wherever you go has always been in my core.

Where else have you had to adapt? After high school, I lived in Barcelona for a little bit and came back to Sweden to study economics. It turned out to be completely wrong for me, so I took my savings and went to New York and started assisting different directors and photographers among other jobs.

When did you realize that economics wasn't the right path? When I moved to New York, I lived in a small apartment with other girls my age that had aspirations and ambitions within the arts and music. I realized that it was okay to try and work for your dream, even if it's outside of a normal everyday job. We encouraged each other a lot and are still good friends today. I started assisting directors, and after a few years I studied experimental film and 16mm film at The New School before applying to Swedish film school.

Why film? For me, filmmaking is a way of communicating, understanding and seeing. I feel very present when I'm filming, like I'm 100 percent there. I also like the whole process of filming and

Right: Theresa wears a coat by Acne Studios.

Photograph: Boe Marion, Styling: Martin Persson

"Fame itself is not something I strive for, but I would like my films to be seen."

then, afterward, sitting and editing. There are so many layers with film—the sound, the music, picture, editing, characters and locations. The possibilities are endless.

Do you prefer to work alone or collaborate? I used to do everything on my own. I still do on smaller projects, but in this current one with more than 170 hours of material, it's been great to have a small crew to work with. It's been good to work with a photographer and editor that I really, really trust.

Do you work better at night or in the morning? I get more done at the beginning of the day.

Do you remember the moment, person or film that inspired you to become a filmmaker? My mother was a teacher and would borrow a VHS camera from her school over the weekend. That was the first time I saw a camera. When I look at those tapes now, I can hear myself in the background pleading to hold it. I've always had an urge to document, to film and take pictures. I guess I feel like I can freeze a moment and take it with me forever—it's like collecting moments. But making a film is so different from just documenting everyday life. I remember watching Fassbinder, Maya Deren or Wiseman films and old documentaries like *Grey Gardens* for the first time. There are so many stories to tell and so many ways to touch magic with film.

What's the worst job you've ever had? I've been working since I was 13 years old, doing all kinds of extra jobs—at a candy shop, restaurant, real estate agency, as a janitor, gardener, guide, kindergarten teacher, TV host. The list is long. The worst job was working at an amusement park and not being allowed to talk to the other workers. Whether I like a job or not comes down to the people I work with and the work environment.

Are there any small, boring tasks that you secretly enjoy doing? I enjoy setting the table and peeling potatoes.

What do you admit to being bad at? Remembering names.

Your last documentary, 'Taxi Sister', also featured women working with cars. Is there a theme in your work? With *Taxi Sister*, the protagonist made a really major choice to become a taxi driver and go against the grain of what was expected of her as a woman. At the mechanic school in the movie I'm currently working on, they didn't get to make that choice. I found it really interesting just to follow the girls in those different worlds. There are so many questions—about becoming a woman, boyfriends and relationships. There are so many things happening and then, on top, there is a layer of doing something that a lot of people have issues with. They go through layers of truths and expectations of how a woman really should be at school, at home and in public.

What do you think about the representation of women in film more generally? I want to see more of it.

Would you ever like to be famous? Fame in itself is not something that I strive for, but I would like for my films to be shown and my exhibitions to be seen.

What are some of the things you miss about Burkina Faso when you're in Sweden, and vice versa? When I'm in Sweden, I miss the red dust, mangoes, the way everyone talks to each other wherever they go, the sounds at night and, of course, my family. When I'm in Burkina Faso, I miss coffee, the four seasons—or all seasons but winter—and, of course, my family and friends.

Left: Theresa wears a top by Yohji Yamamoto and a jacket by Acne Studios.

Photograph: Boe Marion, Styling: Martin Persson

2

Features

Glyptotek

Words by Tristan Rutherford & Photography by Anders Schønnemann

At Copenhagen's Glyptotek, one expects the collection of classical antiquities and French and Danish masters to come alive in the early hours—for the bust of Nero to leer after Degas' *Dancer*, or for Gauguin's *Tahitian Woman* to square off against van Gogh's *Landscape from Saint-Rémy*, as the two masters may once have done following a glass of pastis. The Glyptotek tells the tale of 10,000 different objects. Here, from sarcophagi to sculptures, the weight of history hangs at every turn. A statue of Pompey looks on with ill-disguised conceit, thrilled that his rival Julius Caesar was stabbed to death at his feet; nearby, fellow Roman emperor Caligula still appears disheartened that his statue was thrown into the Tiber by his citizens; elsewhere, a hundred disembodied heads goggle like onlookers in Elysium. Visitors can, in fact, visit the museum after hours. "Slow Evenings" are held once per month, with interactive themes that have thus far covered time, power, boundaries, yearning, desire, madness, death and decay, through lectures, films, music, discussions and dinners.

For instance, the recent death-themed event included a burial ritual by Taiwanese performer Ying-Hsueh Chen, a talk about ghost research by Swedish composer Carl Michael von Hausswolff and a communal dinner of veal fricassee served in its own grave.

Perhaps the first story that needs to be told is that of the museum's creator, Carl Jacobsen—the Danish classicist who paired a passion for ancient art with extraordinarily deep pockets (his father founded the Carlsberg brewing empire). After acquiring his first Greek sculpture, the *Rayet Head*, Jacobsen continued to purchase mummies, tablets, jugs and mugs until, by 1882, his winter garden contained more sculptures than plants. The Danish public was invited to peek inside and a de facto museum was born.

By 1887, however, more viewing galleries had been added by Vilhelm Dahlerup, the Haussmann-meets-Hadid of his day, to house the Glyptotek's French and Danish art collections. A few years later, Jacobsen asked Danish architect Hack Kampmann to create another space for his classical antiquities: a four-winged neoclassical palace sharing artworks from Pompeii to Palmyra in a series of grand galleries.

A century later and the Glyptotek has acquired its own legends. "A visit to the chamber with our Egyptian mummies is spooky," says Flemming Friborg, the museum's director. "The long descent into this room has a dramatic effect, like entering a real tomb. We've had visitors fainting—especially when they discover one of the mummies' fingers sneaking out of the linen bandages."

The Egyptian area of the Kampmann Wing hosts the museum's oldest works. There's Ramses II holding hands with creator god Ptah, proving to all Egypt that king and god are one and the same. The magic eyes daubed on the tomb of Nekhet-Kawi allowed the late Egyptian to see into the land of the living. Her gaze now follows you around the room.

The artistic timeline from Egypt flows into Ancient Greece. An Etruscan urn is adorned with a sphinx. There are artifacts from Italian tombs, where chariots, shields, weapons and incense were buried along with the dead. Just as Greece copied the culture of Egypt, Rome then mimicked Greece. Portrait statues of prominent Romans are clad in Greek togas to hint at old money sophistication. Note the sculpture of Anatolian earth mother Cybele, who was later adopted by the Roman state as part of its own hegemonic cult.

Respite is offered at the café in the Winter Garden between the two wings. A soaring dome shelters palm trees, ferns and creepers. Fountains pouring over sculptures are reminiscent of Tivoli Gardens or Versailles.

Left: The god Apollo, c. A.D. 150, is shown with a lyre and the sacred snake, Python.

Right: Relief sculptures from the Greek and Roman Sculpture exhibition.

> *"Darker salons host the gaunt, twisted, tied and frigid figures that hail from the colder north. Theirs is a tale of mythology and morality, of dark nights and frozen dawns."*

According to Danish architect Louis Becker, who helped design the area, the inspiration was drawn directly from the museum's collection. "Our painters from icy Scandinavia crossed the Alps into Italy to be overwhelmed with wine and beautiful women," says Becker. "So our staircase that leads to the new extension walks visitors up into the light like the ascent to Italy's mountains, warmth and sunshine."

Visitors are guided to these stairs, which lead around the museum to the roof terrace. Now, it's de rigueur for all new Glyptotek employees to stroll up the staircase and kiss the statue of a goddess at the top.

Through neoclassical granite columns and past Renaissance salons, the Dahlerup Wing, the oldest section of the Glyptotek, is dedicated to French and Danish art. The poised poses of Degas invite study, the lusty curves of Rodin suggest laughter and love. Jacobsen became bewitched by Rodin at a French exhibition in Copenhagen in 1888 and ended up buying 24 sculptures directly from the artist. The Glyptotek's current collection of 43 pieces is unique outside of France.

The Danish sculptures are more Nordic. Darker salons host the gaunt, twisted, tied and frigid figures that hail from the colder north. Theirs is a tale of mythology and morality, of dark nights and frozen dawns, not the playful sensuality of the Canova sculptures that soak up the sun in the neighboring salons.

Refreshingly, the Danish Golden Age completes the artistic timeline with a return trip to Rome. Eckersberg, Købke, Hansen and Bendz colored their canvases with inspiration from trips to Italy: Capri, Venice, Naples, Pompeii. In *View of the Via Sacra*, Eckersberg encapsulates the *bel paese en plein air*. Hansen's *Resting Model*, lounging on a divan, was modeled not in Copenhagen but in the sultry half-light of Rome.

A last tour by the security guards and the Glyptotek closes for another day. All the exhibits can now come out to play.

Left: The museum's French and Danish sculpture wing is an exploration of the human body.

Right: 'Winged Female Demon', 6th century B.C., from the Greek and Roman Sculpture exhibition.

Personality Tests:

A Brief History

Aristotle thought that the shape of your ears revealed your innermost psyche. BuzzFeed suggests that it hinges on your favorite Disney princess or pizza topping. From warfare to psych wards to the workplace, *Harriet Fitch Little* uncovers our long-standing fascination with personality tests.

Without categories, the world would be a bewildering jumble of unrecognizable objects. When we encounter something new—a chair, a tree, a dangerous situation—we know what it is because it looks like something we've seen before. As it is with chairs, so it is with people. We plot their extroversion, their compassion, their neuroticism in relation to others—a million tiny signals that coalesce into the thing we label personality. Today, personality tests have simplified, and monetized, this complex calculation. At interviews, assessment centers and team bonding events, testing is ubiquitous. Matchmakers and their online equivalents entice us with the promise that every question answered will bring us one step closer to unlocking our perfect partner. Some devotees even turn to personality tests when making important life decisions. "It was like I'd pulled up the blanket over the universe and looked at God," says Kaila White, an American journalist, recalling one questionnaire that seemed eerily predictive. "It was just so easy to know what [the test taker] would be like as a person."

What is personality? F. Scott Fitzgerald came close to our contemporary understanding in *The Great Gatsby* when he described it as "an unbroken series of successful gestures"—a person's predictable patterns of behavior over time. But perhaps he was toying with his 1920s readers, mocking them for their optimistic belief that science was on the brink of making the stranger's mind knowable; for all his "successful gestures," Gatsby remains an inscrutable stranger.

Almost 100 years on, we are little the wiser as to the fundamental building blocks of personality. And despite recruitment and dating companies building billion dollar industries on the back of the conviction that they can extract some core identity from our heads, the question of how best to test for particular traits remains unresolved.

In ancient Greece, things were simpler: Personality was believed to be a physical thing. Aristotle thought it could be identified just by looking at someone's face. "Men with small ears have the disposition of monkeys, those with large ears the disposition of asses," he wrote in *Physiognomics*, a text in which animals are inventively anthropomorphized to explain human character traits: "The best breeds of dog have ears of moderate size." Hippocrates was slightly subtler, believing personality to stem from an imbalance in the body's four "humors": blood, yellow bile, black bile and phlegm. Anatomical problems required surgical solutions. Bloodletting—one of many unpleasant techniques—was frequently used to restore the balance between the humors: Creating (and then lancing) blisters was thought to release the buildup of the melancholy-causing black bile.

Over two millennia after Hippocrates, the most popular tests still relied on the belief that personality manifested itself physically. Phrenology, the invention of Viennese physician Franz Joseph Gall, advocated the reading of head bumps. The practice was rooted in a theory that different parts of the brain were associated with different personality traits. In particularly active areas, the brain's muscular exertions would push a bump up through the skull. Gall had determined that intelligence was located in the brow region, criminal tendencies clumped behind the ears and "amativeness" (sexual desire) was at the nape of the neck. The great American poet Walt Whitman was among the most fervent advocates of what he termed this "new science" (today, "pseudoscience" might be considered a more appropriate term). Whitman was so flattered by his own reading, which deemed him eloquent, just and in possession of excellent critical faculties, that he published his test results at the front of early editions of *Leaves of Grass* as proof of his greatness as a poet.

Like so many innovations, it was the exigencies of war that forced this fledgling industry to mature. "The very first questionnaire came about at the time of the First World War," says Mark Parkinson, a founding member of the Association for Business Psychology. "Then there was another batch during the Second World War, which was all about recruiting soldiers into the American army."

The first of these newly standardized tests was a simple yes/no check box questionnaire called the Woodworth Scale of Psychoneurotic Tendencies, designed to identify soldiers susceptible to shell shock after the First World War. Its probing was not subtle: The statement "I drink a quart of whiskey every day" was intended to identify the alcohol dependent, while "I believe I am being followed" was used to pinpoint the paranoid. Writing in *The Cult of Personality Testing*, the American author Annie Murphy Paul highlights the irony of this being widely considered the first modern personality test: The symptoms of shell shock were so extreme and so baffling, she writes, that "doctors diagnosed these as cases of 'lost personality.'"

The link between personality testing and pathology endured long after the bombs stopped falling. Psychology was battling to establish itself as a serious branch of empirical science, in particular of medicine, and as such its priority was diagnosing mental illness.

One of the most influential tests developed between the wars was devised on the psychiatric ward of a university hospital in Minnesota. Its creators, Starke Hathaway and John McKinley, had been impressed by Woodworth's system for identifying shell shock, and set out to create a similar test that could diagnose a wider spectrum of disorders. The Minnesota Multiphasic Personality Inventory (MMPI), first published in 1942, consisted of a staggering 504 questions intended to identify everything from depression to schizophrenia. Some of the statements were as obvious as Woodworth's, but many were eccentric and hard to fathom: "Everything is turning out just like the prophets of the Bible said it would"; "My mother was a good woman"; "I liked *Alice in Wonderland*, by Lewis Carroll."

Almost as quickly as new tests were being created they were being seized upon by industry. Business was booming, companies were expanding rapidly and managers were finding themselves fielding many of the same concerns as clinicians about the mental state of their employees, who were now so numerous as to make personal relationships impossible.

The check box tools of hospital diagnoses fit seamlessly into this new landscape of corporate bureaucracy. The creators of the MMPI were quick to assert that the test could be used for assessing normal personalities as well as psychological illness, writing in 1951 that "although the scales are named according to the abnormal manifestation of the symptomatic complex, they have all been shown to have meaning within the normal range." Even Woodworth's shell shock indicator found a ready home, rebooted as the Woodworth Personal Data Sheet.

Already, tests were being invented directly for industry. An incident in an American factory where an employee snapped and killed his boss led directly to the creation of the Humm-Wadsworth Temperament Scale in 1935—a personality test aggressively marketed to businesses with the promise that it could "forestall undesirable behavior through an understanding of unfortunate tendencies." Rather like Hippocrates' humors, the Humm-Wadsworth posited that all personalities risked veering toward one of four extremes: schizophrenia, epilepsy, hysteria and cyclodia (what we would now call bipolar disorder).

Of course, not all personality test developers found it so easy to monetize their insights. In the 1920s, at the same time as Woodworth was testing his shell shock inventory, a Swiss psychologist named Hermann Rorschach was touring psychiatric wards, presenting patients with a series of ambiguous drawings that looked like ink blots and asking them what they saw. He noticed that when he showed the cards to schizophrenic patients in his care, their responses were confused: Where others saw butterflies and flowers they saw an amorphous whirl of menacing figures, sharp objects and dangerous animals. Rorschach went on to create the first widely used projective personality test—an assessment based on the belief

that when presented with ambiguous stimuli, respondents will project unconscious information onto it.

The psychoanalyst was personally skeptical about the test's validity as a predictive measure, but his work was taken up by ardent disciples in the US, who believed not only in its accuracy but also in its ability to identify normal personality traits as well as schizophrenia. Shortly after the Second World War, the test was given to Nazi leaders at the Nuremberg trials. Hermann Göring, the founder of the Gestapo, saw men with red hats where there should be none, indicating "an emotional preoccupation with status."

Other projective tests would follow, including the Thematic Apperception Test, which asked participants to make up scenarios based on pictures cut from magazines, and the Blacky Pictures Test, a storytelling exercise that used cartoon illustrations of dogs to decipher Freudian personality traits such as castration anxiety and penis envy.

John Hunsley, a Canadian psychologist who is currently compiling the second edition of *A Guide to Assessments That Work*, says that there is little indication that projective testing has any validity. "Everyone has, at some point on a nice summer day, been lying with friends on the lawn, looking at clouds floating by and saying what they see in the clouds," he says. "There may well be influence of personality on what people see but there are loads of other things— if you're hungry you're more likely to see food in the Rorschach cards than if you've just had a meal."

Projective tests are still used by some clinicians, particularly in the diagnosis of children, but they never found a grip on industry in the same way that pencil and paper questionnaires did: too expensive, too time-consuming and too hard to standardize. According to Annie Murphy Paul, employees also proved extremely resistant to the storytelling exercises because it wasn't clear what criteria they were

being measured against: Seemingly innocent answers might accidentally reveal some hidden pathology. "The first lesson of projective testing is that we are not as we seem," she writes.

By the late 1950s, concerns about privacy were also threatening the ubiquitous questionnaire. Books with scaremongering titles like *The Brain Watchers* and *The Tyranny of Testing* found large audiences. The most influential of them, William Whyte's *The Organization Man*, railed against the supposed objectivity of workplace assessments: "The process should not be confused with science," he wrote. "When tests are used as selection devices, they're not a neutral tool; they become a large factor in the very equation they purport to measure." The MMPI came under particular scrutiny for its blunt probing into sex, religion and politics. After congressional hearings in the US in 1965 and 1966, its distributors were obliged to scale back some of its more invasive lines of inquiry.

More difficulties arose the following decade, when a growing number of psychologists started to question the fundamental orthodoxy that personality was predictive of behavior.

"Often it is not so much the kind of person a man is as the kind of situation in which he finds himself that determines how he will act," announced Stanley Milgram in 1974. Milgram's name was already synonymous with the most notorious exposition of this theory. Through a series of what he termed "experiments in obedience" conducted at Yale University, he had demonstrated that, when instructed to do so by figures of authority, the majority of people would deliver potentially lethal electric shocks to strangers.

But by the time psychologists were starting to question the discipline, personality testing had escaped their jurisdiction. In the summer of 1966, *Cosmopolitan* started publishing personality quizzes—a regular feature whose prescriptive advice would be integral in defining the "Cosmo Girl" as an aspirational role model for young women. ("Mostly 'A's? Try hinting

"Gall had determined that intelligence was located in the brow region, criminal tendencies clumped behind the ears and 'amativeness' (sexual desire) was at the nape of the neck."

at your sinful side rather than revealing it full on.") That same year, a journalist at *Look* wrote "Boy…Girl…Computer," an in-depth feature that heralded the arrival of computer match-making as the savior of a lovesick generation: Machines could now "tie up college couples with magnetic tape" just by running their personal preferences through a machine.

"If personality tests had remained under the aegis of science, they would never have become beloved on the enormous scale they are today," says Evan Kindley, the Los Angeles–based author of *Questionnaire*, published earlier this year, which charts the explosion of "the form as form" in the 20th century.

John Hunsley agrees. Flicking through the draft pages of *A Guide to Assessments That Work* as evidence, he emphasizes that personality tests have almost totally disappeared from clinical usage. "The focus now is on measuring psychiatric variables that are much more narrowly defined and much more relevant to assessing and treating mental disorders than broad-based personality assessments," he says.

It is a reflection of this transition that the most famous, most widely used personality test in circulation today was created by Katharine Cook Briggs and Isabel Briggs Myers—a mother and daughter duo with no formal training in psychology, who were purportedly motivated by nothing more than a desire to better understand Katharine's enigmatic husband. The Myers-Briggs Type Indicator (MBTI) sorts people into 16 categories along four metrics modeled loosely on Carl Jung's theory of types: intuition/sensing; introversion/extroversion; feeling/thinking; perception/judging. Critically, unlike the measures derived by clinicians, there is no such thing as a "bad" Myers-Briggs personality. The 16 types are different but all equally valuable.

Few psychologists consider Myers-Briggs an accurate gauge of personality. Roughly half of repeat test takers are assigned to a different personality type the second time they take it, and there is little evidence that the types accurately predict behavior or workplace performance. Its success is widely credited to the Barnum effect—our tendency to accept positive personality assessments as true, even when the information is so vague as to be worthless. But skepticism has not dented the test's popularity. By the time of Isabel Myers' death in 1980, it had sold a million copies. Today the test makes around $20 million a year and is used by over 80 percent of Fortune 100 companies. It also boasts a huge community of devotees who consult Myers-Briggs types when making decisions about relationships, conflicts and important transitions. "The goal is to heal people," says Meredith Howell, who co-hosts the popular *When Myers Met Briggs* podcast with her friend Kaila White. "The goal is to help people be their best self."

"In a way, people think of it as a free form of therapy," says Evan Kindley. "[The logic is] I'm not going to go and pay a therapist to figure out who I am—I'll just take a test and then I'll know."

Meanwhile, psychologists have arrived at a workable detente within their field, accepting that personality and situation both have an impact on behavior. "What we're saying when you respond to a questionnaire is 'on balance, you're probably like this,'" says Mark Parkinson, adding cautiously, "but you might not be like that."

The most popular academic theory of personality is currently the Big Five model, which posits the existence of five traits: openness to experience, conscientiousness, extroversion, agreeableness and neuroticism. It's a cautious schema. Critics call it "the psychology of the stranger" because it avoids the extreme pronouncements of its predecessors: There's no mention of mental illness or unconscious trauma, and no invasive lines of questioning.

Many workplace personality tests now model themselves on the Big Five, although there's little consensus on the correct way to identify the traits. "It's a bit like baking a cake," says Parkinson, who devises new tests for businesses. "We all vaguely agree on the ingredients but not on how you might mix them together."

In the continued absence of scientific certainty, why do personality tests hold such sway?

Kindley, who describes us as "both more suspicious and more careless" with our personal information than at any point in history, believes that their appeal is down to a heady mix of rationalism and narcissism. "We like thinking about ourselves, and we also like to believe that science, or data or very smart people have designed some test that will help us learn about ourselves," he says.

Perhaps there is something comforting in being assigned a "type": a celebration of our individuality, but within the predefined parameters of normality.

In our quest for certainty, questionnaires might soon see their supremacy challenged. The company Karmagenes, which launched last year in Geneva, offers a DNA test which it claims can measure 14 personality traits including "bon vivant," "optimist" and "sex-driven." Echoing the Myers-Briggs rhetoric, the site reassures potential test takers that "No one has a better or worse type of genes, it is the diversity that is crucial." Jason Rentfrow, a professor of psychology at the University of Cambridge, says that while he is currently "very skeptical" about the ability of such tests to accurately map an individual's DNA, he is confident that the science will progress to a point at which they can offer real insights into personality: "Eventually we'll get there, in which case why waste your time administering a survey when you could just do a cotton swab and be done with it."

After a century of searching for the right algorithm to unlock personality, the Grecian belief that the mind can be read from the body is once again in ascendance—only now we put our faith in saliva swabs and not in the shape of our ears.

Byr

Ben Gorham's nose is big business. By following it, he's expanded his fragrance brand *Byredo* into a global empire with a new store in Manhattan and a lucrative line of luxury goods. But Gorham was once an outsider in the world of beauty. A tall, tattooed and hard-working guy from the suburbs of Stockholm, Gorham tells how he built his business on nothing but gumption, good taste and a desire to bottle the essence of green beans.

Words by Pip Usher & Photography by Lasse Fløde

edo

"If only there could be an invention that bottled up a memory, like scent. And it never faded, and it never got stale. And then, when one wanted it, the bottle could be uncorked, and it would be like living the moment all over again."

Almost eight decades after Daphne du Maurier first published this idea in her novel *Rebecca*, Ben Gorham has managed to achieve just that. Armed with a notebook, the founder of Swedish fragrance brand Byredo jots down his experiences and feelings as they occur. Later, many of those scrawls end up as fragrances neatly stocked on shelves around the world—fleeting thoughts that he tries, quite literally, to bottle up.

Take his latest perfume, which looked to the bloody battlefields of World War One for inspiration. Based on a story passed on by his tattoo artist, the fragrance, named Rose of No Man's Land, is a floral-scented tribute to the nurses who served on the front lines. Rescuing wounded men who fell in the treacherous no man's land between the trenches, these women provided medical care to soldiers regardless of which side they fought on. In commemoration, many of the men tattooed an image of a nurse on their bodies once they returned home.

"I thought it was a beautiful story of a selfless act," says Gorham of his perfume, which has top notes of pink pepper and Turkish rose petals. "And I thought a fragrance would be a good way to tell the same story." It's a compelling insight into the process that transforms anecdotes drifting through Gorham's mind into the products seen in Byredo collections, sold at retailers that include Harrods, Colette and Barneys. But it's also a glimpse into Gorham himself—a man whose collection of tattoos (so numerous that he's "lost count") includes a nurse in a starched cap, inked across his chest.

Born to an Indian mother and Canadian father, Gorham made

"A lot of my work has fictional components, but it touches bigger notions like love, loss or death."

the improbable transition from professional basketball player to perfumer after founding Byredo in 2006. Despite his lack of formal industry training, Gorham's idea rapidly metamorphosed from a passion project into a global empire: Today, Byredo is sold in 45 markets and has expanded into leather goods, scented candles and a sunglasses collaboration with Oliver Peoples. In 2015, Gorham opened his second brick-and-mortar outpost in New York City's Soho, to join the brand's flagship in Stockholm.

"Routine is a terrible, terrible word for me because I'm on and off airplanes so much," he says. He's just landed back in Sweden after a last-minute trip to New York, and he sounds tired: There are "a hundred other things" he's working on. It's a punishing schedule dictated by the scale of his ambition. "I have a hard time slowing down," he admits. "It's always this exploration of new ideas and products and things."

Byredo's headquarters—formerly those of the Swedish postal service—reflect the loftiness of Gorham's aspirations. An elaborate, dark green fireplace sits opposite generously proportioned windows that welcome in Sweden's scant sunlight. The ceilings are high; polished wooden wainscoting lines the walls. It's a potent symbol of Gorham's ascension from a boyhood spent in the outskirts of Stockholm (which he describes as "pretty poor, generally, lots of people in small apartments, lots of kids hanging out on the streets") to a man sitting at the nucleus of his city's fashion and design scene. "The level of ambition, it's always been there," he says.

The sense of grandeur could also, one suspects, serve as a visual testament to Gorham's dogged pursuit of the ultra-luxe. While Byredo began as a perfume brand, the business is now a conduit through which Gorham can express ideas and experiment with new interests. When he began to feel

Above: Ben's tattoo artist inspired his latest fragrance, Rose of No Man's Land, a floral-scented tribute to the nurses who served on the front lines of World War I.

confined by the beauty framework, he turned his personal obsession with leather into a business. Now, one of Byredo's camel-colored calfskin wallets retails at $500; handbags sell for thousands.

"It was nice to add something to the process that I knew nothing about," he says with a self-effacement that continues throughout the interview. "It was nice to have that feeling of only seeing possibilities again."

Byredo, its name inspired by the Old English word redolence, or agreeable fragrance, seems to mirror the sweetly scented life of Gorham himself. There's the rags-to-riches tale, the striking good looks and impeccable taste. If Gorham has demons, he manages them with the same iron will that has governed much of his life, first as an athlete and now as an entrepreneur. His success, he believes, comes from an "obsessive, non-stop, improving, evolving character that I think you have to possess."

As a kid growing up in the suburbs, with an absent father and a mother determined to keep her son out of trouble, Gorham's first enduring obsession was basketball. Recalling how he used to dribble a ball to school each day, Gorham says the sport was a vehicle through which he could define himself. It was "the only thing I wanted to do and the only thing I was good at," he remembers.

When he was 12 years old, Gorham's mother remarried and the family relocated to Toronto. There, Gorham was forced to confront some profound and unsettling differences in the way his new home viewed him.

"Even though Canada is tolerant and multicultural, there was still this notion of race that was very new to me," he says, the curious timbre of his voice reflecting the years spent bouncing between North America and Europe. "In Sweden, you were either Swedish or a foreigner and that was the only divide. But here it was dissected into smaller groups."

As an entrepreneur, Gorham's diverse background has proved an enormous asset. The sleek modernity of Byredo's branding references Scandinavian design, for example, while scents with notes of cardamom and incense nod to time spent in India with his mother's family. Yet as a teenager transplanted into a new culture, he re-members only a sense of needing "to figure things out."

Throughout the tumult, basketball remained constant. A sports scholarship at Ryerson University was followed by a return to Europe in the hope that he could play professionally. After fruitless struggles with the Swedish government for a passport that would entitle him to sign professional contracts, Gorham gave up his sports career. "I started to realize that it may not happen and, even if it did, I was at an age where the years of playing professionally were limited," he says. "I made a decision to take all that energy and all that ambition and do something else."

And so Gorham took his six-foot-five frame to art school. A life built on physicality was replaced with the more intangible world of creativity: painting and sculpture, history and photography. When he sat next to famed perfumer Pierre Wulff at a dinner party one evening, a conversation about Wulff's line of work proved the impetus for the next decade of Gorham's life.

"I met this guy and learned that smells, which I knew nothing about, were extremely powerful

"I have a thousand ideas about smells—it's really become a way that I see things."

and could be used to evoke emotion in a very interesting way," Gorham says. At the time, he was unemployed and living on a friend's sofa. "I feel fortunate that somebody believed in my ideas and was willing to finance them," he says without elaborating.

Gorham pursued Wulff, traveling to his office in New York to ask for assistance. He then recruited renowned perfumers Olivia Giacobetti and Jérôme Epinette to translate his ideas into scents. His first fragrance, based on an essence of green beans that he remembers smelling on his father as a child, was deeply sentimental. Throughout the experience, Gorham processed some of his own emotional history.

"A lot of my work has fictional components, but it touches bigger notions like love or loss or death," he says. "But when that fragrance got to a certain point, it was like my dad was standing in the room."

How does one convey their father's scent to a perfumer who has never met, let alone smelled, him? Without the vocabulary of a perfumer, Gorham has been forced to get creative; over the years, his briefs have consisted of imagery, words, poetry and music. Lately, as his knowledge of the industry deepens, he has started to include raw materials.

"I try to get the perfumer to understand where I want to go," he explains of a process that takes the fragrance from abstract idea to tangible product. "He creates a first version that is either close enough to the idea that we can modify it and reach the goal, or we throw it out, start again and I have to rewrite the brief." He adds, "I have a thousand ideas about

"I learned that smells were extremely powerful and could be used to evoke emotion."

smells—it's really become a way that I see things. Formulating that in a way that the perfumer understands is a large part of my work."

It can take up to six months before the first iteration of a scent is ready. But the modifications can be an even lengthier process, with Byredo doing anywhere from 30 to 200 modifications on one fragrance. They know when to stop, Gorham says, because "it's an emotional process so you feel when it's done."

As Byredo mushrooms into a global brand, Gorham has come to accept that the business now has a responsibility that reaches far beyond his own needs. "I realized that we're a commercial establishment that makes products for people," he explains. "I didn't engage in that thought for a very long time. I was self-indulgent—I was just making these products for myself. It was just me, me, me for a very long time. I started to realize that people were connecting with these products on an emotional level and that people were spending a lot of money. It made me feel some responsibility in my work, even though it's just perfume or just a bag."

Alongside these responsibilities, Gorham's life has been turned upside down since the arrival of his two daughters; one is seven years old and the other is 18 months. "I've grown more in the last seven years than in the previous 32," he confesses. For him, fatherhood has fulfilled "all of the cli-chés of not being the most important person in your life, how you react and prioritize things, even in how effective you are." Pausing to think, he adds, "I'm a pretty goofy guy, especially around my kids."

His family's home is "filled with old objects and furniture from places [he has] visited." A fan of mid- and late-'60s Italian design aesthetics, he treasures the Ultrafragola mirror by Ettore Sottsass that hangs in his hallway. Another collector's item, the Screen 100 by Finnish designer Alvar Aalto, adds clean Scandinavian lines. But while he values art and sculpture, Gorham's home is more relaxed, more nostalgic, than the sharp minimalism of his brand. "Since I travel so much, staying home in Stockholm is a true luxury," he says.

On weekends, he and his family, in typical Scandinavian style, retreat to their country house in an archipelago just a 25-minute drive from Stockholm. There, they gather with friends and family, enjoying each other's company amid Sweden's striking landscape.

"It's right on the ocean so you swim or go to the sauna or paddle," says Gorham of his country pursuits. "It's a really simple life, but very fulfilling." Despite the frenetic demands of his business, Gorham tries to bring these values of simplicity into every area of his life. He limits the hours he works and the business trips he takes away from his family. When he is home, he focuses on being pres-ent so that his life "becomes less of a juggle and more of a balance."

Consumed by the intellectual challenges of leading a business, Gorham has recently returned to what he knows best: exercise. "I missed the physicality of the life I lived, so I've started running and lifting and boxing and wrestling and climbing and surfing and paddling and skiing," he says. "There's something quite meditative in that for me." With a wry note creeping into his voice, he adds, "I'm trying to figure out if it's some midlife crisis."

As a teenager in Toronto trying to figure out who he was, Gorham did experience a crisis. A decade later, the identity he'd constructed was shattered all over again when he quit basketball. But these days, his life has many facets to it: that of an entrepreneur, leader and family man. It's a sturdy foundation, one built to weather more than a newfound obsession with sport. As for his tattoos, he admits that the pain gets "worse every year"—although that hasn't stopped him.

That's the thing about Gorham: not much does. The tattoos continue to be inked, the business keeps growing, his ideas—so abundant that he jokes they're "part of [his] curse"—are corked and distributed around the world. "You have to believe in yourself," he says. "You have to realize that you'll probably get knocked down 10 or a hundred times. It's as much about getting up as it is about moving forward."

Right: The first fragrance that Ben created was based on the scent of fresh green beans he remembered from his father's garden.

Eyes of the Skin:

Architecture
and the Senses

"I dwell in the city and the city dwells in me," *Juhani Pallasmaa* writes in *The Eyes of the Skin: Architecture and the Senses*. Meandering through phenomenology—the philosophical study of experience—Pallasmaa argues for a holistic architecture, one that considers not only the way spaces look, but the way they feel; for haptic qualities that quicken the pulse, for silence that brushes the nape of one's neck or, as excerpted here, for spaces that impact all five senses of the human body.

Silence, Time and Solitude

The most essential auditory experience created by architecture is tranquillity. Architecture presents the drama of construction silenced into matter, space and light. Ultimately, architecture is the art of petrified silence. When the clutter of construction work ceases, and the shouting of workers dies away, a building becomes a museum of a waiting, patient silence. In Egyptian temples we encounter the silence that surrounded the pharaohs, in the silence of the Gothic cathedral we are reminded of the last dying note of a Gregorian chant, and the echo of Roman footsteps has just faded away from the walls of the Pantheon. Old houses take us back to the slow time and silence of the past. The silence of architecture is a responsive, remembering silence. A powerful architectural experience silences all external noise; it focuses our attention on our very existence, and as with all art, it makes us aware of our fundamental solitude.

The incredible acceleration of speed during the last century has collapsed time into the flat screen of the present, upon which the simultaneity of the world is projected. As time loses its duration, and its echo in the primordial past, man loses his sense of self as a historical being, and is threatened by the terror of time. Architecture emancipates us from the embrace of the present and allows us to experience the slow, healing flow of time. Buildings and cities are instruments and museums of time. They enable us to see and understand the passing of history, and to participate in time cycles that surpass individual life.

Architecture connects us with the dead; through buildings we are able to imagine the bustle of the medieval street, and picture a solemn procession approaching the cathedral. The time of architecture is a detained time; in the greatest of buildings time stands firmly still. In the Great Peristyle at Karnak, time has petrified into an immobile and timeless present. Time and space are eternally locked into each other in the silent spaces between these immense columns; matter, space and time fuse into one singular elemental experience, the sense of being.

The great works of modernity have forever preserved the utopian time of optimism and hope; even after decades of trying fate, they radiate an air of spring and promise. Alvar Aalto's Paimio Sanatorium is heartbreaking in its radiant belief in a humane future and the success of the societal mission of architecture. Le Corbusier's Villa Savoye makes us believe in the union of reason and beauty, ethics and aesthetics. Through periods of dramatic and tragic social and cultural change, Konstantin Melnikov's Melnikov House in Moscow has stood as a silent witness of the will and utopian spirit that once created it. Experiencing a work of art is a private dialogue between the work and the viewer, one that excludes other interactions. "Art is memory's mise-en-scène" and "Art is made by the alone for the alone," as Cyril Connolly writes in *The Unquiet Grave* (1944). Significantly, these are sentences underlined by Luis Barragán in his copy of this book of poetry. A sense of melancholy lies beneath all moving experiences of art; this is the sorrow of beauty's immaterial temporality. Art projects an unattainable ideal, the ideal of beauty that momentarily touches the eternal.

Spaces of Scent

We need only eight molecules of substance to trigger an impulse of smell in a nerve ending, and we can detect more than 10,000 different odors. The most persistent memory of any space is often its smell. I cannot remember the appearance of the door to my grandfather's farmhouse in my early childhood, but I do remember the resistance of its weight and the patina of its wood surface scarred by decades of use, and I recall especially vividly the scent of home that hit my face as an invisible wall behind the door. Every dwelling has its individual smell of home.

A particular smell makes us unknowingly re-enter a space completely forgotten by the retinal memory; the nostrils awaken a forgotten image, and we are enticed to enter a vivid daydream. The nose makes the eyes remember. "Memory and imagination remain associated," as Bachelard writes; "I alone in my memories of another century, can open the deep cupboard that still retains for me alone that unique odor, the odor of raisins, drying on a wicker tray. The odor of raisins! It is an odor that is beyond description, one that it takes a lot of imagination to smell."

What a delight to move from one realm of odor to the next, through the narrow streets of an old town. The scent sphere of a candy store makes one think of the innocence and curiosity of childhood; the dense smell of a shoemaker's workshop makes one imagine horses, saddles and harness straps and the excitement of riding; the fragrance of a bread shop projects images of health, sustenance and physical strength, whereas the perfume of a pastry shop makes one think of bourgeois felicity. Fishing towns are especially memorable because of the fusion of the smells of the sea and of the land; the powerful smell of seaweed makes one sense the depth and weight of the sea, and it turns any prosaic harbor town into the image of the lost Atlantis.

A special joy of travel is to acquaint oneself with the geography and microcosm of smells and tastes. Every city has its spectrum of tastes and odors. Sales counters on the streets are appetizing exhibitions of smells: creatures of the ocean that smell of seaweed, vegetables carrying the odor of fertile earth, and fruits that exude the sweet fragrance of sun and moist summer air. The menus displayed outside restaurants make us fantasize the complete course of a dinner; letters read by the eyes turn into oral sensations.

Why do abandoned houses always have the same hollow smell: Is it because the particular smell is stimulated by emptiness observed by the eye? Helen Keller was able to recognize "an old-fashioned country house because it has several levels of odors, left by a succession of families, of plants, of perfumes and draperies".

In *The Notebooks of Malte Laurids Brigge*, Rainer Maria Rilke gives a dramatic description of images of past life in an already demolished house, conveyed by traces imprinted on the wall of its neighboring house:

There stood the middays and the sicknesses and the exhaled breath and the smoke of years, and the sweat that breaks out under armpits and makes clothes heavy, and the stale breath of mouths, and the fusel odour of sweltering feet. There stood the tang of urine and the burn of soot and the grey reek of potatoes, and the heavy, smooth stench of ageing grease. The sweet, lingering smell of neglected infants was there, and the fearsmell of children who go to school, and the sultriness out of the beds of nubile youths.

The retinal images of contemporary architecture certainly appear sterile and lifeless when compared with the emotional and associative power of the poet's olfactory imagery. The poet releases the scent and taste concealed in words. Through his words a great writer is capable of constructing an entire city with all the colors of life. But significant works of archi-

tecture also project full images of life. In fact, a great architect releases images of ideal life concealed in spaces and shapes. Le Corbusier's sketch of the suspended garden for a block of flats, with the wife beating a rug on the upper balcony, and the husband hitting a boxing bag below, as well as the fish and the electric fan on the kitchen table of the Villa Stein-de-Monzie, are examples of a rare sense of life in modern images of architecture. Photographs of the Melnikov House, on the other hand, reveal a dramatic distance between the metaphysical geometry of the iconic house and the traditionally prosaic realities of life.

The Shape of Touch

"Hands are a complicated organism, a delta in which life from the most distant sources flows together surging into the great current of action. Hands have histories; they even have their own culture and their own particular beauty. We grant them the right to have their own development, their own wishes, feelings, moods and occupations," writes Rainer Maria Rilke in his essay on Auguste Rodin. The hands are the sculptor's eyes; but they are also organs for thought, as Heidegger suggests: "[the] hand's essence can never be determined, or explained, by its being an organ which can grasp [...] Every motion of the hand in every one of its works carries itself through the element of thinking, every bearing of the hand bears itself in that element [...]."

The skin reads the texture, weight, density and temperature of matter. The surface of an old object, polished to perfection by the tool of the craftsman and the assiduous hands of its users, seduces the stroking of the hand. It is pleasurable to press a door handle shining from the thousands of hands that have entered the door before us; the clean shimmer of ageless wear has turned into an image of welcome and hospitality. The door handle is the hand-

"There is a strong identity between naked skin and the sensation of home. The space of warmth around a fireplace is the space of ultimate intimacy and comfort."

shake of the building. The tactile sense connects us with time and tradition: Through impressions of touch we shake the hands of countless generations. A pebble polished by waves is pleasurable to the hand, not only because of its soothing shape, but because it expresses the slow process of its formation; a perfect pebble on the palm materializes duration, it is time turned into shape.

When entering the magnificent outdoor space of Louis Kahn's Salk Institute in La Jolla, California, I felt an irresistible temptation to walk directly to the concrete wall and touch the velvety smoothness and temperature of its skin. Our skin traces temperature spaces with unerring precision; the cool and invigorating shadow under a tree, or the caressing sphere of warmth in a spot of sun, turn into experiences of space and place.

In my childhood images of the Finnish countryside, I can vividly recall walls against the angle of the sun, walls which multiplied the heat of radiation and melted the snow, allowing the first smell of pregnant soil to announce the approach of summer. These early pockets of spring were identified by the skin and the nose as much as by the eye.

Gravity is measured by the bottom of the foot; we trace the density and texture of the ground through our soles. Standing barefoot on a smooth glacial rock by the sea at sunset, and sensing the warmth of the sun-heated stone through one's soles, is an extraordinarily healing experience, making one part of the eternal cycle of nature. One senses the slow breathing of the earth. "In our houses we have nooks and corners in which we like to curl up comfortably. To curl up belongs to the phenomenology of the verb to inhabit, and only those who have learned to do so can inhabit with intensity," writes Bachelard. "And always, in our daydreams, the house is a large cradle," he continues.

There is a strong identity between naked skin and the sensation of home. The experience of home is essentially an experience of intimate warmth. The space of warmth around a fireplace is the space of ultimate intimacy and comfort. Marcel Proust gives a poetic description of such a fireside space, as sensed by the skin: "It is like an immaterial alcove, a warm cave carved into the room itself, a zone of hot weather with floating boundaries." A sense of homecoming has never been stronger for me than when seeing a light in the window of my childhood house in a snow-covered landscape at dusk, the memory of the warm interior gently warming my frozen limbs. Home and the pleasure of the skin turn into a singular sensation.

Spaces of Memory & Imagination
We have an innate capacity for remembering and imagining places. Perception, memory and imagination are in constant interaction; the domain of presence fuses into images of memory and fantasy. We keep constructing an immense city of evocation and remembrance, and all the cities we have visited are precincts of this metropolis of the mind.

Literature and cinema would be devoid of their power of enchantment without our capacity to *enter* a remembered or imagined place. The spaces and places enticed by a work of art are real in the full sense of the experience. "Tintoretto did not choose that yellow rift in the sky above Golgotha to signify anguish or to provoke it. It is anguish and yellow sky at the same time. Not sky of anguish or anguished sky; it is anguish become thing, anguish which has turned into yellow-rift of sky," writes Sartre. Similarly, the architecture of Michelangelo does not present symbols of melancholy; his buildings actually mourn. When experiencing a work of art, a curious exchange takes place; the work projects its aura, and we project our own emotions and percepts on the work. The

melancholy in Michelangelo's architecture is fundamentally the viewer's sense of his/her own melancholy enticed by the authority of the work. Enigmatically, we encounter ourselves in the work. Memory takes us back to distant cities, and novels transport us through cities invoked by the magic of the writer's word. The rooms, squares and streets of a great writer are as vivid as any that we have visited; the invisible cities of Italo Calvino have forever enriched the urban geography of the world. The city of San Francisco unfolds in its multiplicity through the montage of Hitchcock's *Vertigo*; we *enter* the haunting edifices in the steps of the protagonist and see them *through* his eyes. We *become* citizens of mid-19th-century St. Petersburg through the incantations of Dostoyevsky. We *are* in the room of Raskolnikov's shocking double murder, we *are* among the terrified spectators watching Mikolka and his drunken friends beat a horse to death, frustrated by our inability to prevent the insane and purposeless cruelty.

The cities of filmmakers, built up of momentary fragments, envelop us with the full vigor of real cities. The streets in great paintings continue around corners and past the edges of the picture frame into the invisible with all the intricacies of life. "[The painter] makes [houses], that is, he creates an imaginary house on the canvas and not a sign of a house. And the house which thus appears preserves all the ambiguity of real houses," writes Sartre.

There are cities that remain mere distant visual images when remembered, and cities that are remembered in all their vivacity. The memory re-evokes the delightful city with all its sounds and smells and variations of light and shade. I can even choose whether to walk on the sunny side or the shaded side of the street in the pleasurable city of my remembrance. The real measure of the qualities of a city is whether one can imagine falling in love in it.

Hot Under

When the temperature drops, take shelter against the dreary days and cold nights with winter essentials.

the Collar

Photography by Hasse Nielsen & Styling by Carolyne Rapp

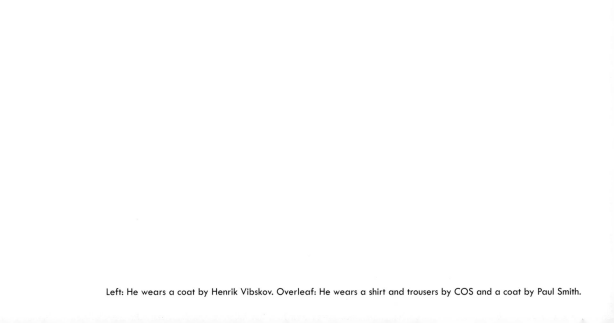

Left: He wears a coat by Henrik Vibskov. Overleaf: He wears a shirt and trousers by COS and a coat by Paul Smith.

Left: He wears a jacket and trousers by Margaret Howell. Above: He wears a coat by Sandro and trousers by Z Zegna.

Left: He wears a shirt by COS, coat by Wooyoungmi and trousers by Acne Studios.

Above: He wears a shirt by Tonsure, coat and trousers by Lanvin and shoes by COS. Right: He wears a shirt by Acne Studios and coat by Issey Miyake.

Left: He wears a shirt by COS and coat by Wooyoungmi.

Above: He wears a coat by Acne Studios. Right: He wears a sweater and coat by Acne Studios and trousers by Tom Wood.

Day in the Life:
Stine Goya

Stine Goya has been a quiet presence in the fashion world for more than a decade—first as a model, then as an editor, now as a designer. Softly spoken and strong-minded, Stine has developed her business thanks in part to her admirable respect for life outside of it. *Words by Julie Cirelli & Photography by Lasse Fløde*

Stine Goya—Denmark's redheaded fashion entrepreneur and sweetheart of the '70s silk pantsuit set—has little trouble commanding attention. Without raising her voice above the decibel level of a murmur, she makes a striking impression. Stine's been at the helm of her eponymous womenswear line for 10 years and has more than 30 collections under her belt, and though she speaks softly and laughs easily, her demure manner belies a fearsome business acumen. Stine has much to share of what she's learned about the growth of a healthy business over the last decade and that asking for what you want is no easy task, nor is relinquishing control.

Where are you from? I grew up in a very small town outside of Copenhagen called Taarbæk. When I was a child, it was just a little fishing village, though it's grown into a wealthy enclave since then. Taarbæk is close to the sea and dotted with small cottages surrounded by forest. I had a very safe, calm childhood. Everything seemed like it was just around the corner, and we'd take a lot of walks to the harbor to look at the sea. My parents brought me up in a very traditional way.

What is a "traditional upbringing" in Denmark? My family's values were very old-fashioned: My parents taught me to take care of myself and to be polite and independent. I was the youngest of six children, and we were all expected to work for our own money and to contribute to the family—to help clean up the table after dinner, that sort of thing.

My parents were reserved, but also open and lively. They had an active social life, and I would go with them when they went out. I never had a babysitter, I just followed along to dinners and sat listening to their voices. They always included me, and I contributed to the family. I try to teach these things to my sons, who are two and five years old.

What other kinds of things from your childhood do you find yourself incorporating into raising your own children? Of course there are always things you want to do differently, but even so, you often end up doing the same things your parents did. I try to raise my kids with good manners, but I also think it's important to try to instill a sense of self-confidence and to gently push them into doing things that they're good at. That's something my parents have always done for me: They showed me that they believed in me. Even when I chose a direction in life they couldn't relate to, they remained open to it and never told me to take a more traditional path. They could have easily discouraged me, since I was a little bit of a lonely rider when I was younger. I've always been quite shy.

You started modeling after you finished studying at Central Saint Martins in London. Did your shyness make it difficult for you to be the center of attention? Modeling was strange for me, because I had always been this little pale kid who was teased for my red hair. Then suddenly, in London, they thought I looked cool because I had an androgynous look. But the whole time I was modeling, I thought that any day now they would find out that I was not actually pretty.

I had never dreamed of being a model, so I had a built-in distance from it. But it was an interesting experience. I got to go behind the scenes in the industry and I saw so many things from the inside: I saw how to build up a fashion show and the different ways large and small companies operated. There were a few companies that I worked with for quite a while. It was helpful to follow their progress and see how they developed and adapted the way they worked over time. I learned a lot of things that I later applied to my own business.

You returned to Denmark to become fashion director of *Cover* magazine. What happened next? When I first returned to Denmark, I worked so much. I worked until three o'clock in the morning every day. I had all these assistants running around, and we were constantly pressed by deadlines. It was an exciting challenge, but not sustainable in the long term. After a year, I decided it was time to start my own company. I wanted to use my education to start a brand that didn't exist in Denmark at that time. I was a bit naive going into it—I had no idea what kind of challenge I was facing. Maybe that was a good thing.

Left: Stine serves as an ambassador for Denmark's Ordrupgaard Museum. Olafur Eliasson's sculpture *Vær i vejret* (Weather the Weather) is part of the museum's outdoor Art Playground.

> *"I expect a certain percentage of failure in every project, and that's okay.*
> *Even if things don't go my way, I have to stay calm."*

That was in 2006, and you presented the first collection in 2007. What did it look like? It was very colorful and playful. I think even my first collection had a signature—something that made people think, "Wow, what is this?," you know? From the beginning I have collaborated with a Danish or international artist on conceptualizing one print for each collection. For me the process of designing around the artist's print is a welcome interruption to my everyday work. It was part of my original approach 10 years ago and is something I continue today.

You've refined that signature over the last decade. How was the current collection conceived? The most recent collection is inspired by a book I found in an antique shop called *The Cloud Spinner*. It's the story of a boy who can weave clouds into fabric. His mother warns him not to weave too much, only what is needed. One day, he is sitting on a hill, weaving, when the king asks the boy to weave him a tapestry. The moral of the story is that even though the clouds bring rain, the rain is needed. And if you remove all of the clouds, there will be no rain and subsequently, no food for the kingdom. It is an excellent metaphor for sustainability and the transient ways of the fashion industry.

Is sustainability important to you? It's something we think about a lot and that informs our perspective. Being sustainably minded in the fashion industry is particularly difficult for small companies, but one of the things we can do is concentrate on making collections that are long-lasting and stand outside the trend cycle. Approaching this idea through the current collection—through the narrative of the cloud spinner—is a playful way to take on a massive, serious issue.

You have a fast-paced job with a lot of responsibility. How do you stay centered, so you aren't knocked around by the world? Going from being an entrepreneur to running a proper business has been a major transition for me. But you learn with the years to take some things a bit more calmly. I'm a super-perfectionist; I don't want to show anything I'm not proud of. But now I'm experienced enough to know that some things are just not going to work. I can expect a certain percentage of failure in every project, and that's okay. I can't let myself freak out, because if I did it would create a very bad energy for the rest of the company. Even if things don't go my way, I have to stay calm.

Are there other things you've learned as your business has grown? As we've matured into a more professional company, I have had to learn not to be so in control of everything. I used to know everything that was going on in my business. My challenge is delegating some of that responsibility to others. I have to trust that I have good people around, and just make myself let go. I've also had to learn to make decisions based on facts instead of feelings.

Left: Stine often wears pieces from her own collections, which are recognizable for their liberal use of color and pattern.

Does that mean that you sometimes have to say no to yourself? Right. I can't just go with the flow anymore and do whatever I feel. I have to think strategically and stick to the brand's DNA. It's really easy to be influenced by people and be pushed about. In the past, I've followed the advice of others to move away from the core values of the company and it's gone badly. As my company has grown, I've also had to learn how to communicate what I want. Early on, I used to do so many things myself, but now I have to be able to express to other people what I want them to do and how they should work. It's something that takes practice.

Do you remain connected to your business day and night? Do you check your email first thing in the morning and at night before you go to bed? I don't allow myself to check my email when I'm home with my kids, because I only get a few hours with them every day. When I go to bed I might check my phone, but I never reply at that hour—I just make sure there are no disasters.

Does your family like to cook and eat together? We always eat together. It's very important to us to have a time when we all sit down. Breakfast is the nicest time of the day, because everyone is calm and we can talk about what should happen during the day. We never skip breakfast together.

What is the day like after breakfast? These days, I usually take my kids to school on my bike—one in the front and one in the back—then continue on to work. Before I had kids I always walked from place to place, because even though Copenhagen is such a bicycling city, I love the pace of walking, and I love to think and sort out problems in my mind as I walk.

Do you have a place where you can just shut the world out and concentrate on yourself? My dream is to have more time to myself. When I do, I like to take a swim in the ocean, even in the winter. I go to a beautiful old wooden bathhouse north of Copenhagen to take a sauna and swim in the cold sea. To go from extreme heat to icy water cleans the mind and makes me feel extraordinarily calm.

A DARKER UNIVERSE
Stine Goya x Kähler

This fall, Goya is set to release a collection of vases and planters in similar hues of pale pinks, midnight blues, golds and creams as her garments. The collection is a collaboration with 175-year-old Danish ceramics brand Kähler, an institution in Danish design. The 12-piece series of billowing shapes, named Fiora, is Goya's interpretation of 1960s stoneware. *Available from Kähler Design, Copenhagen, in November 2016.*

3

Work

Occupational

A uniform has the power to command something of its wearer and, in turn, from the world.

Hazards

Photography by Zoltan Tombor, Styling by Alpha Vomero & Uniforms by Hakuï

Previous page: (Left Model) She wears a top by Steven Alan and dress by Hakuï. (Right Model) She wears a top and dress by Hakuï.

Left: She wears a jacket by Hakuï. Above: She wears a shirt and jacket by Hakuï, and a coat and trousers by Samuji.

Right: She wears trousers by Hakuï and shoes by Creatures of Comfort.

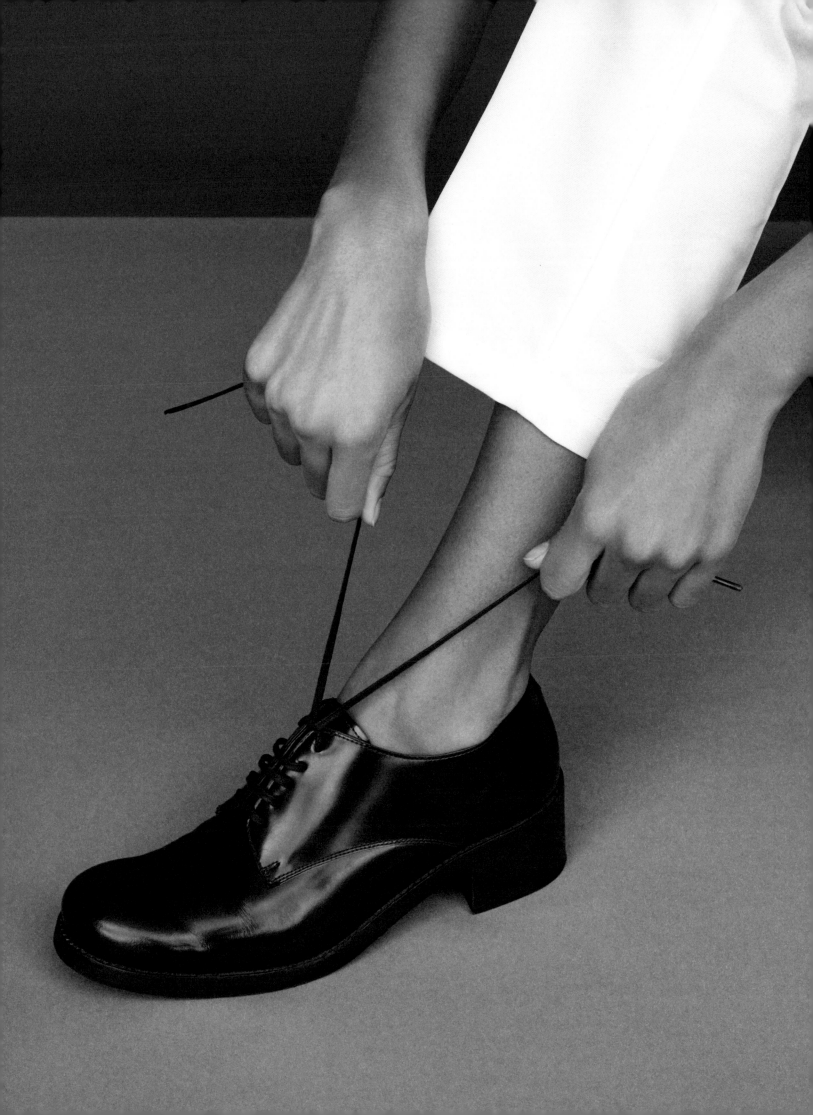

Above: (Left Model) She wears a top by Steven Alan and dress by Hakuï. (Right Model) She wears a top and dress by Hakuï.

Above: She wears a top and trousers by Hakuï, coat by Steven Alan and shoes by Creatures of Comfort.

Above: She wears a top by Hakuï, trousers by Sea New York and shoes by Creatures of Comfort. Right: She wears a shirt and apron by Hakuï.

Above: She wears a turtleneck by Steven Alan, top and pants by Hakuï and shoes by Common Projects. Right: She wears a vintage jacket and a chef's coat by Hakuï.

Previous page: They wear tops by Hakuï. Above: She wears a top and trousers by Hakuï and coat by Sea New York.

Above: She wears a top by Samuji, jacket by Hakuï, trousers by Steven Alan and shoes by Rodebjer.

Left: She wears a top by Creatures of Comfort and coat by Sea New York.

In Conversation:
Group Dynamics

You can choose your job, but you can't choose your colleagues. For better or worse, dynamics in the workplace can be a delicate ecosystem. To learn how to manage conflict and grow more attuned to one another, we invite leadership coach *Kari Uman* and clinical psychologist *Murray Nossel* to advise on collaborating more constructively. *Words by Molly Rose Kaufman*

Please tell us about yourselves and how your work relates to group dynamics in the workplace. Kari Uman: I'm a leadership coach, and I frequently work with women who are being promoted or who are starting a new job or position. Many women hold onto myths about how to be a leader—for instance, that working hard will automatically get you a promotion. Workplace values have radically changed in recent years, and I help individuals cope with these changes.

Murray Nossel: I'm a clinical psychologist with a Ph.D. in social work and anthropology. In the '90s, I evolved a listening and storytelling methodology to teach people how to connect with one another. My company, Narativ, applies this methodology to a business setting. When I started Narativ in 2006, it was unheard of to share personal stories at work. People said to me, "Are you nuts?" But in 2016, the landscape has completely changed. People recognize that sharing and listening are important strategies for connecting and building trust within a group or organization.

How do sharing and listening build trust? Murray: My method holds that there is a reciprocal relationship between listening and telling. Let's say that there is something going on in a team that everybody knows about, but no one is talking about—for instance, someone is going to be laid off. What are people on the team experiencing? Fear, paranoia. They might start feeling competitive with other people because they wonder who is going to be next. The lack of transparency breeds suspicion. What kinds of stories are going to be produced in that environment? Paranoid and fearful stories.

If you want to get people to communicate with one another in a way that is generative, creative and open, you have to teach them how to listen to one another without judgment. This is particularly difficult in a competitive environment because people are trying to survive and they feel like their survival depends on climbing on top, dominating or competing with someone else.

Are there strategies that a leader can employ to encourage open communication? Murray: You can't expect intimate conversations to happen spontaneously in the course of day-to-day discourse. You have to create a dedicated time and space. You also have to give people very specific guidelines on how to listen and talk to one another. It comes more easily with a little bit of guidance.

Kari: Everybody rolls their eyes when you encourage them to share their personal experiences at work. "Why do we have to talk about feelings?" Well, the reason we talk about feelings is that when people feel they are being heard, they are more likely to develop trust.

One of the things that I train people to do is to actively listen. If a listener is really present, nothing else is going on in their head. They are not trying to come up with a witty response. They are paying attention to the content of the conversation. When you listen in this way, you paraphrase the content that somebody has told you, and you also clarify and help them acknowledge their feelings.

Active listening is about helping people get clear on their feelings and then move beyond them. I often tell people that they might as well talk about how they feel because their feelings are written all over them anyway.

Murray: Most people have difficulty expressing their feelings openly. It's scary to let the lid off personal storytelling—people are terrified that some Pandora's box will open and there will be a free-for-all of emotional expression.

Kari, you mentioned outdated tropes in the workplace, that many people—women, particularly—feel that hard work is enough to get you promoted. Could you elaborate? Kari: Getting ahead within the workplace—within any group—is not just about hard work, or even good quality work. Networking, getting out of one's office, taking risks, being proactive—these are the qualities that get you promoted. Success is predicated on building healthy relationships because ultimately people want to work with people they like. This goes doubly for women, who from an early age are often taught to be polite, soft-spoken and compliant, and to put the health of the rela-

tionship above their individual needs. These behaviors run counter to those that actually move people ahead in the workforce.

Do you observe differences between how each generation approaches these notions? Kari: Yes. I do a lot of work in the federal government, where you have boomers [ages 52-70] and millennials [ages 19-35] working together. Millennials are often better at being assertive in the workplace. Women from older generations were taught not to toot their own horns, but the younger generation has learned the value of standing up for themselves and taking credit for their accomplishments. I think that shows real progress.

Does the changing economy influence how people relate to each other at work? Murray: The workplace is like any other communal setting, but it's bogged down with inherited conversations and antiquated narratives. One of the inherited conversations is this idea of efficiency. The industrial revolution produced a relationship to the manufacturing of goods in which the human body was equated with a machine. What you wanted to get out of the human body was maximum efficiency with minimum breakdown.

The problem is that we no longer live in a manufacturing economy. We live in an informational and service economy in which the human being—the being, the beingness of humanity—is now the vehicle. Our imaginations, our ability to innovate and our ability to solve

"Getting ahead in the workplace is not just about hard work, or even good quality work. Success is predicated on building healthy relationships, because ultimately people want to work with people they like."

problems are the requirements of today's workplace. We're not meant to simply function like machines. So we're applying these antiquated, obsolete messages from the industrial revolution to the way that companies work today. It's time to move on, and to recognize the collective intelligence that exists in a company.

Is it possible to shift dynamics that seem entrenched? Murray: I'll answer with a story. In 2005, I went back to my hometown of Cape Town, South Africa. I was hired to do a workshop that ended up being totally packed with people. One man had come all the way from the Transkei—a 600-mile journey—because he was the storyteller in his village. Some women started to tell their stories, mostly to do with family members dying of AIDS. Most of the women in the room were crying. I asked people to reflect on the stories that had been told and the man said, "This is the problem with women: They are weak. They cry at the drop of a hat." The women got angry and started to tell him off.

I asked the women to form a circle around the men, and for the men to form a group inside the circle of women. Then I asked the men to tell stories about what it is to be a man. The man who had offended the group of women told his own story. He had grown up in a very rural area and his father was a goatherd. He had looked after goats since he was five years old. He went out barefoot and stayed with the goats the whole day while the girls in his family went to school. So from that, he concluded that girls were weak because they couldn't

be goatherds and went to school and needed shoes, while he went without shoes and school. As he told his story, the women's relationship to him changed. What had sounded like a sexist remark was totally altered. They were able to develop a tremendous empathy for the life he had lived.

And then, of course, I got the men to sit in a circle around the women and listen to their stories of what it meant to be a woman. You can create those kinds of atmospheres when people are willing to listen to one another through sharing their personal narratives. They come to a deeper understanding of one another that is not based on reaction or judgment.

Do you think personal sharing helps teams to work better together? Kari: When people open themselves up, they are sharing generally from the heart. And that's where the empathy comes in. It's heart-to-heart, instead of head-to-head. Once people connect to each other, they are less fearful of being in conflict. When people trust each other, only then can they truly engage in constructive conflict. High-performing teams need to be able to have conflict and discuss things. And if they cannot manage conflict at all, then a commitment to the mission or the objective flies out the window.

If you do not have the commitment, then who is accountable to whom? Ultimately, it all falls apart. Organizations end up with teams that have a great deal of conflict, a lot of stuff not being talked about. But usually, it *is* talked about in small groups—over a drink, in the

bathroom, in pairs. Amazing conversations happen in the bathroom, instead of around the table where they should be happening.

Murray: How can we possibly imagine a world in which people are able to talk to one another across divides—ancient conflicts, sometimes—if we cannot even do it in our own relatively safe, relatively contained groups? I work with people to identify what gets in the way of their ability to listen to one another. If we come to our relationships with a whole bunch of assumptions, judgments and opinions that are already formulated, then we're never really open to finding out who other people really are. We're listening to everything through the lens of our own preexisting filters.

I'm training people to take a good look at what those filters are and to be ruthlessly honest about how they truly see things. What are the cognitive and emotional habits they use when viewing other people?

When you can examine how you're listening to people, then people are much freer to tell their stories. In my training, teaching people how to listen to one another is always the prerequisite for teaching people how to open up to one another.

What is a corporation if it is not a community of people? A corporation is like any community, and that community of people can choose how they are going to relate to one another and how they will solve problems together. It starts with how teams relate to one another. This radiates to the rest of the corporation and then to the rest of the world.

At Work With:
Laurent Martin

A little more than a decade ago, *Laurent Martin* defected from the advertising world. At the age of 50, he developed a monomania that saw him retreat into an artist's life in rural Catalonia. The object of his deep-set and dense fixation? Bamboo. *Words by Pip Usher & Photography by Mirjam Bleeker*

There are late bloomers and then there is Laurent Martin. The sculptor—a sturdily built man with bushy brows that dance across his face—began his "artist's life" at 50 years old. Before that, the first five decades had followed a fairly ordinary path: There was a successful career as a creative director and relocation from his native France to the sunnier climes of Barcelona. He had a son and a daily routine. Then he discovered bamboo.

"It was a revelation," Martin recalls. After becoming intrigued by the interior architecture of Barcelona's first sushi bar, he first split some bamboo to try to simulate its structure. He was immediately obsessed; in 2004, he left behind the "artificial world" of advertising and started life again, this time as a full-time artist. He has made a career of it ever since.

Look at Martin's work and it's easy to understand the appeal of his material of choice. Gracefully curved strips of bamboo circle in arcs through the air, suspended like mobiles so that they can sway with the breeze. Some are comprised of numerous pieces of undulating bamboo, others are elegant in their singular simplicity. But throughout all of his work runs an enduring theme of peacefulness. Bamboo gave Martin a sense of equilibrium—now he wants to transmit that inner calmness to others.

"Bamboo is about balance," he explains. "I'm looking for balance and harmony." As a result, Martin is more interested in the emotional resonance of his sculptures on viewers than any aesthetic ideal. His agent, Mercedes, remembers the first time she saw his work at an exhibition in northern Spain. "When I came into the gallery and saw all these sculptures floating in the air and moving, I was like, 'Wow,'" she says, perched next to Martin throughout his interview. "You have a sense of magic; you are calm. The pieces are in balance and that means they give you a sense of balance."

These days, Martin's quest for tranquillity has led to a simple life; the speed of the advertising industry has been replaced with a pace that mirrors his rustic surroundings. He's relocated to a converted factory in the Spanish countryside that houses his living space and studio. Even the furnishings of his house are sparse and functional, with bamboo floors and a bamboo staircase banister. Martin's quick laughter and expressive face seem like markings of a Mediterranean man. Mercedes suspects that, much like his beloved bamboo, his soul is from elsewhere.

Left: The inherent flexibility and graceful curve of bamboo allows it to sway gently with the breeze.

Right: Laurent leaves sticks of bamboo outside to dry for two to eight months before initiating the construction process.

"The structure of bamboo is like an antenna. It makes you feel calm because it catches all of the noises and vibrations. It cleans the space and the atmosphere."

In 2004, you said goodbye to your old life in the advertising industry and embarked on a journey around the "Bamboo Road" of India and Southeast Asia. What prompted this adventure? When I first started splitting and cutting bamboo [in 1998], I fell in love. I stayed in fashion and advertising for five more years, but by night I worked on this new hobby. I read a lot, and watched things on the internet.

Five years later, I stopped my life in Barcelona. I sold all I could sell and went to Asia to study bamboo behavior and bamboo handicrafts and everything I could learn about bamboo. When I left, I wasn't afraid of anything. I'd discovered a new passion and I went where my passion called me. I had a good job, good friends—but the call of the bamboo was very strong.

The first step was India, then Thailand, Laos and Vietnam. I was looking for people that were really living with bamboo. I wanted to see, to learn, to begin my "Bamboo Story." It was very interesting for me to feel the happiness of people living in villages where the houses are made of bamboo. In Europe, we talk about the prehistoric age; in northern Laos, they talk about the bamboo age. Bamboo was the first material they used to live—to hunt, to fish, to eat, to make a home. It was a very impressive experience.

What is the appeal of the material for you? If you walk through a bamboo forest, you feel a very special atmosphere. Its structure is like an antenna—you feel calm because it catches all of the noises and vibrations. It cleans the space and the atmosphere.

Bamboo is a very connective material. Thomas Edison's first lightbulb was built with the fiber of carbon and bamboo. Once, I was talking on the phone with a man in India and I couldn't hear him. He said, "Don't you work with bamboo?" I said, "Yes," and he said, "Take a piece of bamboo in one hand and then call me." I did it—and it worked!

For me, it's very important to work with natural and sustainable materials. Bamboo is the most sustainable plant on the earth. In Thailand, in India, in China, in parts of the world with bamboo, they talk about it as the material of the future. There are a lot of architects and designers studying the fiber because you can shape it more easily than wood. In areas where there are earthquakes, they use it in structural architecture because it moves, it's very flexible and it won't be broken.

What is the process in creating your sculptures? It's very important for my work that I don't draw. Instead, I follow the structure of the material to create my sculptures. I work with the bamboo's flexibility, resistance and lightness so that the sculptures are built from the material, not my mind. The first thing I'm looking for is the balance point. Then I split most of the bamboo and make sticks. Each piece is very different—you can feel the difference in the fiber. I remove the internal fiber and that's when I choose the flexibility of my sticks.

If you watch bamboo growing, there's a very particular structure because it is composed of knots. Between the knots there's space. That's why the bamboo is a balanced plant: The base is very strong, the middle is flexible for the wind and the top is strong for the leaves.

Once I'm ready for construction, I put the bamboo sticks outside my workshop and let them dry between two to eight months. I can modify the effect of the weather on the fiber. I work a lot with the rain, the sun, the warm air, the cold air. The wind from the mountain is very dry, the wind from the sea is wet and the mixture between these two modifies the shape of my work. The curves it generates are very nice—better than what I can do with my hands. Nature is the best sculptor.

Are you trying to explore something spiritual with your work? The people who understand my work say that it's nice to look at it because it's relaxing. It's not only the aesthetic; there's a lot of feeling within my work. In bamboo, I've found an answer to my own equilibrium and I think I wanted to transmit this sensation of balance. Now I'm doing sculptures I call energy domes. These sculptures aren't just something to see from outside, but from inside too thanks to the atmosphere that they generate. When I first worked inside the dome, I felt a very good energy—very quiet, very calm. When I told my friend, he said, "Yeah, yeah, Laurent—forget it." But two days later, my friend called again and said, "When my dogs saw your energy dome, they made a hole under it and now they sleep inside the dome."

You're originally from Paris, but you've lived in Spain for 25 years now. Why did you decide to settle there? I'm very happy in Spain because of the character of the Mediterranean people. They're more funny, more enthusiastic, than the French. In Spain, I met a way of life, a way of thinking, that enchanted me. When you're an artist—because it's hard, you have to fight a lot—it helps that the people here are optimists.

What has been the most exciting moment of your career so far? The first exhibition, the last exhibition and all the exhibitions in between! The last one was very exciting—it was in Hong Kong and it was my first exhibition in a bamboo country. They received me well.

How do you make sure your studio is conducive to creativity? I like to listen to good music, to be quiet, to be alone, to have good light.

What is your home like? How does it reflect you? I live between Barcelona and the French border. It's a very nice landscape: The sea is beautiful, the light is really special. It's like the Spanish version of Tuscany. There are a lot of painters in this area because the light is so good. These groups of artists are really helpful and easy. There's no competition. I needed a lot of space for my work so I was very lucky to find an old factory. I could do what I wanted for my home and for my workshop. It's a dream home. I feel really good in every part of it. When I eat, I feel good; when I sleep, I feel good. The floor is bamboo and there is a lot of natural light entering the house. It's functional—there is nothing superfluous. It's very simple… And it's very simple to clean! In my bedroom, there's an energy dome above my head. I sleep very well, and I dream very well, too. I like the futon bed—it's on a Japanese-style tatami. My barbershop chair is my favorite place to see my work. I put myself in the chair, I look at my work, I think, I smoke a cigarette. Outside my house, there are pieces of bamboo drying. They're all works in progress. When I finish one, I put it in the showroom because then I have to protect it from the weather. I keep a few secret pieces for me, but not a lot because I like when people buy them—not for the money, but for the work.

Words by Pip Usher

Necessary Evils: Competitiveness Ambition Confrontation Passive Aggression

Sophie Hicks

By leveraging her insider insight and competitive edge, *Sophie Hicks* has become fashion's favorite architect. Here, she discusses how she keeps her competitive impulses in balance.

Photograph: Marsÿ Hild Þórsdóttir, Photography Assistant: Katrín Ólafsdóttir

Left: Competitiveness can be healthy, Sophie says, as long as you don't lose perspective.

Every morning, Sophie Hicks walks across the roof terrace that connects her home to her architecture firm. "That's an odd bit of routine," she confides, dressed in a sharp collared shirt and glasses. Despite living amid the abundance of restaurants and boutiques in London's Notting Hill neighborhood, Sophie remains steadfastly enclosed within, always eating lunch at her desk and then swimming laps in her pool once the day ends. She is, says a colleague, "working while she's walking."

This relentless efficiency has packed a lot into the past four decades. First, there was Sophie's 10-year career in fashion, which included plum jobs as a fashion editor at *Tatler* and *British Vogue* in the '80s. She also acted in a Fellini film, worked as a stylist for her friend Azzedine Alaïa, earned a degree in architecture, had three children and launched her own business while still in the midst of her studies. "It's quite a lot," she says, a model of British understatement.

These days, Sophie has built a reputation as "fashion's architect," her industry experience and eye for detail making her a favorite for luxury brands that include Paul Smith, Yohji Yamamoto and Chloé. When you throw in the successful modeling careers of her two daughters, Edie and Olympia, both of whom have graced countless magazine covers and catwalk shows, and the modeling career of her mother, Joan, in the '50s, it all begins to sound rather glamorous. But, Sophie insists, she did not grow up in that world: "We hardly had a fashion life going on in our house. I was extremely unfashionable as a child, I can tell you," she says.

A childhood dream of being an architect finally materialized when Sophie quit the fashion industry and returned to her studies, designing homes and offices for friends as she completed her degree. Four years later, she embarked on a series of projects for Paul Smith. Shortly after, the rest of the industry came knocking.

"When fashion companies want their office designed, there's a huge gulf between the architect and the designer. Architects are usually quite dry, and the fashion world is totally different," she says. Not only does Sophie successfully bridge this gap, but she taps into her industry knowledge when she creates concepts for her clients.

"When I was asked to pitch for Chloé, while Phoebe [Philo] was there, I could just look at a couple of her collections online and think, 'Okay, I see what she's doing,'" she says of her ongoing collaboration with the French luxury brand. "I could look at Phoebe's clothes and translate it into an environment." Since 2002, Sophie has designed over 100 stores for Chloé worldwide.

Last November, Sophie unveiled her latest collaboration with Acne Studios—a flagship store in Seoul that she's dubbed the "concrete monster." A translucent light box set amid the capital's meandering side streets, it's a beautiful showcase of her "bare bones" approach to design. The building's interior reveals a stark concrete structure and uncompromising lack of decorative finish. Sophie's work often melds this tough aesthetic to an unexpected sense of calm—including her own home, which she describes as looking "bare and unfinished" yet with a surprisingly homey feel.

Sophie says she pays little attention to the work of her peers, although she believes in the power of friendly competition to spur herself on. "When I swim on my own, I flounder up and down the pool," she says of her nightly ritual. "I'm quite lazy about it. When I'm swimming and someone else gets into the pool, I have quite a competitive streak. I swim more lengths, I swim faster and I get much better exercise."

But for all its benefits, she's careful to keep this quality in check. "I think competitiveness is healthy when it's controlled and when you're not doing things purely for emotional reasons," she says. "It makes people up their game, but you can't get out of hand. And you have to not mind when you lose, which is very difficult sometimes. If you invest too much into your competitiveness, you lose perspective."

Charlie Casely-Hayford

If determination is a necessary quality for success, why does chasing our dreams often feel like running in place? Fashion designer *Charlie Casely-Hayford* muses on the double-edged sword that is ambition.

"I think, quite often, what happens in people's minds is that ambition creates an unobtainable goal so there's never a feeling of fulfillment," says British fashion designer Charlie Casely-Hayford. "A lot of people go through life chasing whatever it is that keeps them motivated. If you don't reflect on your achievements, it's very hard to move forward in a positive way."

Perhaps this meditative tendency comes naturally to a man who seems predisposed toward equanimity; or, it could be that his long-term relationship with interior designer Sophie Ashby has introduced in him a more well-rounded attitude. Either way, the 30-year-old, whose eponymous label is designed in partnership with his father, Joe, is careful to temper his personal aspirations with self-examination. In the often brutal world of fashion, it's proved a savvy way to avoid conflict.

"You know, the expression 'people putting you down' is there because it's very rare that there's resentment from people above you or on your level," he confides. "I'm about everyone doing their best. I'm doing my thing, you're doing yours. I've gone through my life like that because that's how my parents brought me up. If people sense that, there isn't as much aggression."

Part of the fashion world since he was in utero, Charlie's life could inspire jealousy from others. His parents met when they were both students at Central Saint Martins. In the years that followed, his father cut his teeth as creative director at Savile Row tailor Gieves & Hawkes while simultaneously developing his own label. In the midst of that, his father was awarded an OBE from the Queen. "I went to fashion shows with my sister as a kid and we had these amazing wardrobes growing up. But I didn't really get fashion so I didn't want to wear the clothes," he remembers. "It's odd growing up as a teenager when your parents are a lot cooler than you."

Despite his parents' considerable influence—not to mention the wider clout of the Casely-Hayford clan, who were named the most influential black family in the UK by the "Powerlist" of Britain's 100 most influential black people in 2008—Charlie's entry into fashion happened at his own pace. "[My father and I] got into fashion for the same reasons, but it happened independently," he says, noting that he had studied art history at university beforehand. "I'm kind of glad about the way it happened. It allowed me to find out that I wanted to go into that world myself rather than because both my parents did it."

Now, father and son work together in a warehouse in Tottenham, a remarkably diverse area of North London. Charlie describes the label as a blend of two worlds—British anarchy meets the nation's more traditional style—and treats each collection as a conversation between the two. Often, his surroundings play muse, with bold, South American-inspired prints or oversized sweaters reminiscent of British grunge cropping up in the duo's collections. "It's wonderful to experience the clash of people going about their lives and interacting in a quite seamless way," Charlie says of his city.

Much like London itself, the Casely-Hayford House continues to evolve. This June, father and son debuted a womenswear capsule collection. And, Charlie says, they plan to move in a more specialized direction, developing a made-to-measure side of the business that he describes as more fulfilling.

"When you design a collection, you never see who wears it," he explains. "It kind of leaves a gap in you as a designer—it leaves you thirsty. I think what's lovely about bespoke is the satisfaction from both sides."

As a family-run enterprise, there's a traditional backbone to the Casely-Hayford brand that's at odds with the capriciousness of the fashion industry. It's a differentiating feature Charlie is proud of. "There's always a sense of integrity in what we do," he says. "It's not just about the clothes: It's more than that. I've learned a lot about myself and my family from designing."

LAW OF JANTE
by Pip Usher

The Law of Jante, first laid out by Aksel Sandemose in 1933 in a satirical novel about small-town Denmark, defined the 10 commandments of belonging in his nation. While the rules vary slightly, the bottom line in each remains the same: Don't get ideas above your station. Social conformity is to be valued over individuality, and the collective good over personal ambition. To break from that is to incite judgment and, at worst, social exclusion. While this code has become specific to the small, tightly knit Nordic countries, a similar attitude is found in cultures across the world. In the United Kingdom, New Zealand and Australia, "tall poppy syndrome" describes the way in which successful people are cut down to size by others envious of their accomplishments. A mentality aiming to encourage conformity at the cost of mediocrity, it's rooted in resentment. And in the Philippines, it's known as "crab mentality"—a phrase that fittingly reflects the 7,000 islands of which the country is comprised. Describing a bucket of crabs struggling to escape and frantically pulling each other back down, it highlights the envy and pettiness that can debilitate a society.

Janina Pedan

There are two definitions of the word "collaborate." One is to work jointly on a project; the other is to cooperate traitorously with an enemy. Set designer *Janina Pedan* discusses personality clashes in the workplace.

Photograph: Marsý Hild Þórsdóttir, Photography Assistant: Katrín Ólafsdóttir

"People wouldn't describe me as smiley exactly," Janina Pedan admits with a small, self-deprecating laugh. The Ukrainian-born set designer, renowned for the hauntingly beautiful visual feasts she masterminds for style bibles like *Dazed & Confused* and *AnOther Magazine*, is a carefully considered voice in an industry often dominated by caricature-like personalities. Just don't expect her to make small talk. "I think people find me nice, but I'm not the most sociable person on set," she adds.

Janina's cool head has proved an inestimable asset. Born in 1984 in the Soviet Union, she moved to London in her early 20s to study fine art at Goldsmiths, University of London, after which she briefly pursued a career in the art world. It was an experience that she would later find invaluable when navigating the egos of the fashion world. "My experience in the art world shaped me," she says, noting the paradoxical melting pot that meshed struggling artists together with the obscene wealth of those collecting it. "Nothing in fashion has shocked me as much."

When a photographer friend asked for help on a fashion shoot, Janina crafted her first set, which, to those unfamiliar with the process, means handling everything from physical labor—creating backdrops or props—to more abstract tasks, like considering concepts and the relationship to the environment. "I'm very influenced by design and sculpture in my work which means I often custom-make furniture and sculptural objects for my sets," Janina explains. "Spending more time in the workshop than in front of the computer is essential to me. I think important creative decisions are made in the process of making an object."

It's this hands-on approach that has ruffled the plumage of many a male photographer determined to micromanage her responsibilities. "My assistants and set builders tend to be women. I usually have a female team that does what may be seen as traditionally male—building sets, using power tools. There's a lot of weird attitude. I get a lot of mistrustful comments or opinions about how we do things."

Janina, whose exquisite eye for detail has brought atmospheric flair not only to fashion shoots but also to the shop windows of womenswear designer Simone Rocha, has always been careful to check her own ego at the door. Soft-spoken and describing herself as stable and calm, she is confident standing up for herself but tries to confront situations without escalating them further. "I'm good at telling people what I think without any drama," she says. "For some people, that's hard to do without it turning into a massive issue." But she admits that it's still difficult to challenge outlandish behavior, particularly in an industry that can operate on the assumption that practically everyone is replaceable. "The main thing I have a problem with is hierarchical attitudes, where people treat assistants as second-class citizens," she explains. "You get some of that in fashion because there's a lot of fictitious power, and sometimes people get really carried away with it... It's hard to negotiate these situations," she adds. "You have to choose your battles." Since her transition into fashion, Janina has worked with *Vogue*, *Harper's Bazaar*, *Vanity Fair*, *The Wall Street Journal* and *Wallpaper* magazine. At this stage, she's a fashion veteran, her freelance schedule allowing her the freedom to pick and choose jobs. As a result, she increasingly explores projects beyond the commercial fashion world, finding the most creative fulfillment through collaborations with her photographer friend Ben Toms.

"Whenever we work on a project together, they're always the most fun because we have shared interests. We explore things outside of fashion and then bring that excitement and interest into producing images," she says.

Over the years, Janina has intentionally gravitated toward collaborating with those who have the same values. It is, she explains, best for her own well-being to be surrounded by colleagues that she respects. "People get a lot of space to behave horribly," she says, reflecting on the fashion world and its tolerance for difficult personalities. "Things are often blown out of proportion."

Left: Soft-spoken and calm, Janina confronts difficult situations without escalating them further.

Philippe Malouin

When Canadian designer *Philippe Malouin* moved to London, he found himself doing business in a nation notoriously too polite to say what it really means. Here, he shares his way to beat beating around the bush.

"My friends describe me as goofy, like a big, dumb dog," says Philippe Malouin as he explains why, when they witnessed his business persona for the first time this summer, they were taken aback. "I was on vacation in July with friends and I had a business call about a product I'm developing in New Zealand. They were all a bit freaked out because they'd never seen me like that," he laughs.

Philippe, an award-winning product designer with his own studio in London, switches from oversized Labrador to a vision of professionalism as soon as it comes to his business. When he's not creating bedside tables, bowls or light installations, Philippe can be found lending a critical eye to the sleekly modern interior design jobs handled by his company, Post-Office, for clients that have included skincare brand Aesop and swimwear label Orlebar Brown. His ethos values simplicity above all else and is driven by a desire to streamline objects down to their most undiluted form. "I like every shape to be dictated by its function. It's as reduced as possible so it looks like what it's meant to do," he explains.

Currently, the bushy-bearded Philippe is working on a number of projects that reflect his diverse abilities as a designer. Glancing at an office wall plastered with his company's projects, he reels them off: a public art installation in America; a show for a gallery in Monaco; a shop design for an Italian leather goods brand. It's little wonder that when he has some free time in his demanding schedule, he often wants to "just stay at home and do absolutely nothing."

If things had gone according to his parents' plan, Philippe would be working at the family's law firm in a small town outside of Montreal. Instead, he set his sights on becoming a professional snowboarder—a dream that was shattered when he grew 13 inches as a teenager and his balance "went out the window"—before shifting his attention to the arts. Several years spent roaming Europe after college confirmed his hunch that an alternative existence was out there, and he's pursued it ever since.

"I'd been exposed to creative possibilities that you don't necessarily encounter in Canada," he recalls of his travels. A bachelor's degree from the Design Academy Eindhoven in the Netherlands followed, its conceptually driven course "totally different to anything [he'd] ever seen." He began interning for British furniture designer Tom Dixon, and his career accelerated very quickly after that. "Working for Tom was the best thing that could have happened to me. I was really green," he says.

By 2009, Philippe had turned his attention full-time to the design studio he'd set up after graduating. Many business owners struggle to manage the insidious passive-aggressive politics that crop up in their workplace, but Philippe's bluntness has always bulldozed any of that away. "I'm very direct and brutally honest," he says. "Sometimes, when I'm working with a client, I can say that something is hideous or awful and I hate it. It's not always tactful, but it's true."

To balance his unfiltered frankness, Philippe avoids tense situations by choosing to work with clients and colleagues with whom he feels comfortable. It's this shared understanding that allows his team to produce their best work. "We do tend to work with clients that we actually like and we do tend to not work with clients that we don't like," he says. "I guess that's how I deal with it. I don't think we're difficult to like, but sometimes it happens. You've got to stay calm and talk about it, but I'm very passionate about what I do and the decisions that we make so I'll fight for them."

As the boss of his own business, Philippe is careful to hire colleagues that mirror his own mentality toward work. "We work way too much to work with people that we don't have a connection with," he explains, adding that he likes to work with people who don't take themselves too seriously. "We're just making bric-a-brac. I don't believe in this whole 'design star, savior of the design world' crap. We're extremely lucky to be doing this for a living. That's enough for me."

THE ART OF RIVALRY
by Pip Usher

Sebastian Smee's novel *The Art of Rivalry* turns an observant eye to the uneasy and influential relationships that existed between some of the greatest painters in modern art. "The art of rivalry is, in this sense, the struggle of intimacy itself: the restless, twitching battle to get closer to someone, which must somehow be balanced with the battle to remain unique," Smee writes. Looking first at the friendship between Lucian Freud and Francis Bacon, Smee reveals the push/pull dynamic which inspired the work of both men. Their friendship was "asymmetrical"; it was dominated by Bacon, the older and more celebrated artist, whose sway over Freud was acute. "Bacon's influence touched everything," Smee says. "If his company triggered many changes in Freud's life, it also triggered a veritable, if slow-burning, crisis in his art. It affected not just Freud's method but also his feeling about subject matter and his fundamental sense of what, for him, was possible." After decades of closeness, the friendship ended in animosity and alienation from one another—the price of rivalry, it seems, that often gets paid.

Nic

Thirty years after founding a fashion label that still bears her name, *Nicole Farhi* walked away and did not look back. Now, in a studio at the bottom of her garden in London, she's channeling all of her creative energy, inimitable style and eye for form and materiality into a robust second act as a sculptor.

Words by Sarah Moroz, Photography by Marsý Hild Þórsdóttir & Styling by Emily Whitmore

ole

What happens when you sell your name? Nicole Farhi, the woman, no longer has any involvement with the brand that still bears her namesake. Following three decades at the helm of a successful fashion label, Farhi walked away in 2012 in favor of transforming an avid hobby—sculpture—into her life's work.

Initially, sculpture was a practice that simply overlapped with design, a pastime that necessarily had to be sidelined so that Farhi could power her business. Today, there is no other activity that can vie for her attention: Sculpture is the sole, impassioned nexus of her life. "This is it. This is what I wanted to do," she says.

Her delight in sculpture is articulated through her devoted routine: She wakes up early and gets into the studio, working mostly on her feet. She pauses to lunch with her centenarian mother, whom she also takes care of full time on weekends, before returning to the studio in the afternoon. When she struggles with a commission for a museum, as she recently has with a bust of English painter Thomas Gainsborough (it fell, and she had to start over), she says: "I'll get there. I'm stubborn."

When we meet, she is dressed in a white crew neck shirt, black trousers and white sneakers: ele-gant in her simplicity. Her hair is free-flowing and wild. Farhi has a gentle manner, but can also be delightfully tart. ("I'll stay online but I would kill myself rather than inflict myself on others," she recently responded to a question from *The Financial Times* about sharing her summer experiences on social media.)

She makes coffee from behind the fully functional vintage bar she brought over from France, reclaimed from a café near Les Halles that she used to frequent in Paris. Alongside strong coffee, she offers some madeleines—a sweet afternoon snack *à la française*.

Farhi lives with her husband, Sir David Hare, an English writer and director. His adapted screenplay for *The Hours* was nominated for an Academy Award in 2002, and he's been behind many Tony Award-winning plays since the 1970s, notably *Plenty*. Farhi's mother lives with them, and the trio resides in Hampstead, in north London. The peaceable environs seem like a context in which one could get serious work done: Hampstead has the ready-to-exhale feel of a retreat. There is very little foot traffic and more noise from birds than humans. The centuries-old houses are of stately brick and boast their own names (Brabourne House, Bay Tree Cottage). The Hampstead Parish Church and a small overgrown cemetery are down the way, each solemn and charming.

Farhi's home is 18th-century Georgian: warm, lived-in and replete with books and art. Overlooking her stairway are small statues and busts dotted along the wall. Sculptures of severed feet are used as doorstops. They were made by Farhi's mentor, Eduardo Paolozzi, a Scottish-born artist with a diverse art catalog. (He is perhaps best known for his bronze sculpture of Isaac Newton in the piazza of the British Library.) He was also instrumental in Farhi's path toward full-time sculpture.

Although renowned for fashion, Farhi has always been attracted to the art world. With the first large amount of money she ever made, she bought a two-level atelier in the 16th arrondissement of Paris. A storied space, it used to belong to French painter and critic Françoise Gilot, Picasso's lover and muse for nearly a decade. Farhi still owns that property, but she now works from a luminous conservatory that runs along the garden in Hampstead, which is partially invaded by a vigorously healthy, blossoming fig tree.

Farhi goes to museums and galleries frequently: "I love to see what people have done," she says. Last year, she was especially seduced

Right: Nicole's 18th-century Georgian home is warm, lived-in and filled with books and art, including sculptures of severed feet by artist Eduardo Paolozzi, which Nicole uses as doorstops.

Photography Assistant: Gwen Trannoy

by a retrospective of the work of Lynda Benglis, a bold and long-practicing artist, who has been dabbling in ceramic sculpture since the 1990s. The two even met up in New York, when Benglis tried to lure Farhi to start a new ceramic practice in her Santa Fe studio. Farhi describes Benglis' work as "colorful and twisted and organic," and says she was impressed by the evocative potential Benglis' ceramics elicited. "I thought, 'This is something I would like to do. I wouldn't do pots, but I would like to do ceramic sculpture.'" Farhi marvels: "It's exciting to see that there could be so much more to explore."

Farhi's debut exhibition as a sculptor was *From the Neck Up*, held in 2014 at Bowman Sculpture in London. Situated between Christie's and the Royal Academy of Arts, the gallery spotlights everything from 19th-century European romantic sculpture (Jean-Baptiste Carpeaux, Albert-Ernest Carrier-Belleuse, Aimé-Jules Dalou) to 20th-century British modern pieces (Henry Moore, Barbara Hepworth). Farhi joined the ranks of that legacy with a 12-piece series of busts of her friends—an inspired entourage that includes Helena Bonham Carter and Anna Wintour.

Now, two years later, Bowman Sculpture is presenting Farhi's second solo exhibition—*The Human Hand*—a single-minded study by way of 24 sculptures. "I really enjoy doing just the limb. I think it's fantastic to concentrate on just one thing. It's small, but means so much," Farhi says. Though the expressions of her busts were intimate and telling, she feels that hands can convey secret, significant things—ones that the face just might convincingly hide.

Farhi made a list of the people that she wanted to depict and their professions, all drawn from the cultural world. These included three pianists, a conductor, a flutist, a violinist, a ceramicist, a painter, and three ballet dancers. It's a celebration of the artisan and the artisanal: people connected to their bodies and to careful craft. Each sculpture is formulated "in the position of their art or profession—they're very expressive of what they do," Farhi emphasizes. She did her research—attending a ballet rehearsal to get the pose for the dancers, going to a concert to hear and observe the pianist—to witness people doing what they excel at.

"It's important to know how it works," she says of learning the hand's bone structure. *Drawing Hands & Feet: Form, Proportions, Gestures and Actions*, the pragmatic how-to by Giovanni Civardi, is among the books on her studio's shelves. "I spent a few months just looking at the anatomy and the place of the hand in the cortex," she says. (The hand is operational thanks to communication between the motor cortex and the cerebellum.) "You don't have to be completely accurate," Farhi says. "You can do what you want. But if I didn't know all the little bones in the wrist, that there is a junction here, and that you have all the articulations in the fingers… " She traces the lines on her own hand to illustrate.

Farhi magnified the hands for symbolic reasons: "I feel that the hand is so much larger than life! It is much bigger than just the action." She explains that the sculpture of her friend Eduardo's bearish paws conveys "much more about what I *felt* about him." He had "padded, fleshy, thick fingers—and at the same time they were soft, and articulate." Emotion trumps realism: "With him, I forgot about the anatomy and wanted to show the power."

Farhi's material choices are deliberate. The ceramicist is cast in glass. For the dancers, Farhi decided to include their arms for the beauty of their musculature. The writer is modeled on her husband, David. An embroiderer, with whom she previously collaborated for her clothing label, was integrated long-distance: he sent photographs of his hands sewing beads onto fabric. The hands belonging to a baker work a phantom ball of dough, and resonate with Farhi's active gestures as she shapes clay. She made the baker's hands white, a wink to flour ("beautiful hands, very soft," Farhi murmurs appreciatively). A glazier is encapsulated in a single thumb, the arch of his finger curved as while applying putty along the edge of a glass pane. Inspired when a glazier came to change a windowpane in her studio, she was in awe at the way his profession had deformed his finger.

Farhi's own hands, with her fingers extended, are cast as a kind of self-portrait. She also cast the hands of her mother, whose age lines from a century of living are extremely poignant to examine.

"Maybe I see things from a little bit farther away—which is a good thing. If you're an artist, you see things differently from most people anyway."

Left: Nicole's second act as a sculptor was a radical—but not altogether unexpected—departure from her life in the fashion industry.

Accompanying the hands of the women are those of a little boy—a budding musician, learning to play the drums. Placed together on a shelf in Farhi's studio, the three sculptures form a moving triptych: the dawn, middle and dusk of life.

In her annex studio—luminous with multiple skylights—Farhi shows me a mood board of hands from different angles. Farhi uses photographs as a work tool and the mood board is a key methodology that carries over from her days in fashion, when she used them "to make sure that everything was different enough, and worked." For her current series, she drew around the hands of each person in the same way that a child might make a drawing of a Thanksgiving turkey from the outline of their fingers and palm.

Photography is also an important component of her exhibition: she collaborated with Walter van Dyk, who photographed each sitter. The portrait images will be shown separately in the gallery, to satisfy any curiosity about who is "behind" each hand. "Who do they belong to? Everybody wants to know who they are," Farhi sighs. "Some of the people who sat are well-known, some are less well-known, but what they do is terribly important," she says. "I didn't want people to come and see the show and say, 'Is this the hand of a famous dancer?' Or, 'Are these the hands of that famous violinist?' I wanted them to just be attracted by the sculpture for what it means—its giving, its softness, its generosity."

Although based in England for her entire adult life, Farhi says,

"Obviously I feel different from English people. I feel very French still." Not just French: "My parents came from Turkey, and my heritage is Jewish Turkish, and from Spain and Egypt. I feel quite fortunate, in a way, to come from so many different places," she notes. "Maybe I see things from a little bit farther away—which is a good thing," she says. "If you're an artist, you see things differently from most people anyway."

Farhi was raised in Nice, the sunny French city on the lip of the Mediterranean. She did not come from an artistic background or family; her father ran a lighting business. She gravitated toward art "probably to be antagonistic, and not wanting to be the same," she concedes. "I went the other way." Her parents liked music, theater and film, but were not compelled by art and "certainly not sculpture." She still returns to Nice to see her brother, who lives in the same building and on the same floor as the painter Henri Matisse once did, even sharing the artist's same view over the city.

Farhi's desire to study art drove her to Paris; she moved there at the age of 18 and lived in an attic apartment. Paris in 1968 was an exuberant time and place for a student, rife with political action and rebellion. To earn money, Farhi sketched drawings of catwalk shows for a fashion magazine. After graduating, she freelanced as a designer for other labels until she met and fell for Stephen Marks, an entrepreneur. "Fashion took over," Farhi recalls. "At the time, in the late '60s, it was easy to start and I wanted to earn a living. It was simple to do it this way."

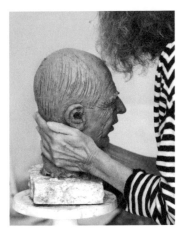

Marks persuaded her to move to London to start French Connection in the early 1970s, and she did. "I wanted to go to America when I was young," she reminisces. "I went to New York for a fashion show with the first company I worked for, Pierre D'Alby. I was totally in love with that town. But I was already working, so I thought that I couldn't start all over again." She founded her eponymous label, Nicole Farhi, in the early 1980s, with the backing of Marks.

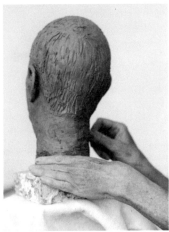

Asked if she sees a relationship between making anatomically correct sculptures and garments that adhere to the realities of the body, she finds the parallel apt, but admits: "There are so many things you don't know consciously that you do!" Of any creative endeavor, she states: "The structure is so important. I need to know what's inside before I do the outside. You need to know the proportions." Still, she feels the overlap between her former life as a fashion designer and her current life as a sculptor stops at the structural level. "I like doing things not for commercial use," she says. "Because I'm older, and I've done one thing, I can afford to do what I'm doing—happily, peacefully," she says. "I never think I'm going to sell so if I do, it's a bonus. Whereas before, if I didn't sell my clothes, it was terrible—it was tragic. It's a different attitude."

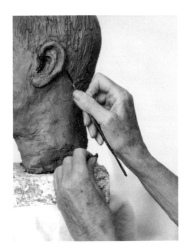

If selling her work is incidental, being part of the conversation is not. "I still want to exhibit my work," she emphasizes of putting her sculpture out there. "I wouldn't want to just sculpt in the dark. I want to hear what people think."

Right: In Nicole's sculpture, the human body is expressed in a variety of forms and media, from a ballerina's slender musculature to busts of Helena Bonham Carter and Anna Wintour.

Tips:
Business Cards
Contracts
Brainstorming
Hiring

Words by Rachel Gallaher, Photography by Aaron Tilley & Set Design by Sandy Suffield

Business Cards

The humble business card. Clocking in at an average of 2 by 3 ½ inches, this small rectangle of card is often treated as a conversational afterthought. Hastily pulled from purses and pockets, business cards frequently change hands only to find their fate at the bottom of briefcases or the back of desk drawers. In the age of email, where technology allows individuals to share information with the tap of an app, the idea of exchanging cards might seem quaint, if not superfluous. But for much of the world, it is a crucial step in establishing professional relationships. Ignoring the expected decorum can leave a poor impression or negatively impact a sought-after deal.

"Business card exchanges are an important sign of your level of professional education and international savvy," says Syndi Seid, a San Francisco–based expert on international business protocol and the founder of Advanced Etiquette, a website that provides tools and information meant to whip us all into polished, polite individuals. "You should always think of a business card as an extension of yourself or an extension of the person offering it and treat it as such. You would never write on a person's face, so you should never write on their card."

With a history rooted in social decorum, business cards are the direct descendants of calling cards, which were used in North America and Europe primarily during the 18th and 19th centuries.

A staple of respectable society, calling cards announced visits and came with a complicated and rigidly adhered-to set of rules. If a card was returned to the sender in an envelope, it meant to keep social distance; folding the upper right-hand corner indicated that the card's owner had personally delivered it; abbreviated lettering often indicated the type of visit, be it congratulatory or commiserative.

While we no longer bend or fold business cards to indicate various messages, there still exists a basic etiquette for swapping contact information. "Asian culture has influenced the world on how everyone is to properly present, receive, keep and use business cards, no matter where you travel," Seid notes. "Following this protocol will ensure you present yourself and your company in a positive way, and help build professional relationships."

So, what are the steps to a successful exchange? According to Seid, they start long before you even meet someone else. "It's important to present a pristine card that isn't creased, smudged or ripped," she says. Keep your cards in a designated case to prevent damage and make sure to always have a sufficient number of cards on hand. If going on a work trip or attending a conference, Seid suggests bringing triple the amount you think you'll need. It's better to carry home any extras than find yourself without one during a crucial interaction.

When presenting your card, *always* use the right hand. (Holding cards out in the left hand is a grave insult, and using two hands shows the highest form of respect.) When accepting someone's card, take a few moments to study it. Compliment the font or logo. Don't immediately shove it into your purse or wallet, and especially avoid putting the card in your back pocket because, as Seid notes, "It's like sitting on someone's face!"

Similar to the pre-exchange prep, your job isn't done after you leave one another. Remember to follow up with an email (or even better, a handwritten note) thanking the person for their time and tying up any loose ends from the previous conversation. It may seem like a hassle, but a postmarked note shows that you truly valued the interaction and it might just be the thing to get *your* card to the top of the pile.

Words by Molly Mandell

Contracts

Signing contracts has become such a ubiquitous fact of modern life that hardly anyone pays it much attention anymore. The contracts required to sign up for relatively benign services like online music streaming are so lengthy and complicated that users are tacitly encouraged to waive fundamental rights or agree to alarming policies. American actor Richard Dreyfuss gives dramatic readings of iTunes' agreements for this very reason.

This contractual blind spot is not lost on music industry insiders. Take, for example, the demands of rock band Van Halen, who required every tour venue to provide a single bowl of M&Ms with "absolutely no brown ones." For years, this provision was interpreted as a symptom of the excessive lifestyle of the rock-and-roll jet set. In his 1998 autobiography,

Crazy from the Heat, however, the band's frontman, David Lee Roth explained that the clause was added for safety's sake. If he saw a brown M&M, he could assume that the contract hadn't been thoroughly read and would inspect other aspects of production for potentially dangerous technical errors.

Formally speaking, a contract is a binding commitment between two parties, both of whom agree to an exchange. Yet the significance of signing a contract may be undermined by the ordinariness of the act, particularly in the digital sphere, where clicking "I agree" seems almost omnipresent.

A 2016 study by researchers at the University of Connecticut and York University illustrates just how infrequently people actually read the forms they sign. Undergraduate students were asked to evaluate NameDrop, a new—although un-

beknownst to them, fictitious —social network. Every single volunteer agreed to NameDrop's terms of service. Only 83 out of 543 participants raised concerns about the clause requiring them to give up their first-born child.

Contract expert and author of *Boilerplate,* Margaret Jane Radin, says that individuals who sign paperwork on a daily basis often fail to read or understand the fine print that they are approving. "People think that a contract is something that can't be amended before it's signed. They don't know that a contract is supposed to be an agreement between people who are free to make changes, something that benefits both parties," she says. In other words, you don't have to sign everything that's put in front of you—especially when it means signing away your unborn children.

Much like "thinking outside the box," "brainstorming" is a piece of midcentury business jargon that ought to be eradicated from the workplace, not least because research shows that the concept behind it doesn't work.

"Creativity is not about having one big blast of insight where suddenly everything becomes clear and the clouds part," says Keith Sawyer, a professor at the University of North Carolina at Chapel Hill who researches creativity, collaboration and learning. "We have all sorts of research evidence that you're better off having everyone do it alone," he says.

This is not breaking news: One decade after Alex Osborne first extolled the benefits of team brainstorming in his 1948 book, *Your Creative Power*, scientists at Yale University had already refuted his claims. Meanwhile, group brainstorming remains the protracted approach to decision-making at the modern office, often under the guise of workshopping or worse, dialogue.

"A lot of people tend to think of creativity as lightbulb moments," Sawyer says. "But good ideas are always combinations of existing mental stuff—all of the things you've ever learned and seen that are floating around in your brain." One might think, then, that freelancers and those working independently would have the upper hand or at least an enviable escape from macro-picture, trigger-pull-ing breakfast conferences. But while group brainstorming sessions may be an ineffective way of generating ideas, groups do have certain advantages when it comes to implementing them.

"The idea of a lone genius is a myth," says Sawyer. Individuals are proven to generate better ideas than groups, but groups are better than individuals at evaluating, selecting and developing those ideas. Groups who work together are better able to connect errant flakes of inspiration to build toward something bigger. "The execution of a good idea is hastened by interaction," says Sawyer. "Groups have the power to bring together ideas and move them forward more successfully."

Brainstorming

Words by John Clifford Burns

Words by Charles Shafaieh

Hiring

Try as one might to make perfect professional choices, hiring involves an inescapable element of risk for employer and employee alike. So long as humans play any role in interviewing, the process—like all exchanges between people—will retain certain unquantifiable and mysterious qualities, just as the outcome of bringing someone new into a company only reveals itself after the job has been accepted.

Faced with this uncomfortable reality, hiring managers around the world and in the United States, in particular, have tried eliminating negative surprises by placing an increased emphasis on "cultural fit"—an amorphous concept that broadly signifies the degree to which a person's attitude, work style and interests align with those of the workplace. The concept itself is not new; all sensitive hiring, even an intentional search for total disrupters, incorporates these criteria to at least a minor degree. In a piece on the practice for the *New York Times*, Lauren Rivera, associate professor of management and organizations at Northwestern University's Kellogg School of Management, argues that "when done carefully, selecting new workers this way can make organizations more productive and profitable."

A far from ideal shift has occurred in its application, however. As Rivera observes, fit no longer principally concerns organizational values but rather the "interviewers' personal enjoyment and fun." Instead of considering a candidate's skills that directly relate to the job, employers are now asking themselves whether they would enjoy being stuck at an airport with this person. Others, like a member of a law firm quoted in the piece, see the hiring process as

akin to dating: "You kind of know when there's a match."

How honest are we in these situations, though? "When we open our mouths to utter descriptions about ourselves to the boss, a coworker, or government official dealing with an unemployment claim, someone else, an alien and foreign semiotic force, begins to speak in our place," Peter Fleming writes in *The Mythology of Work: How Capitalism Persists Despite Itself*, describing "a post-industrial office version of invasion of the body snatchers." But if our interviews are filled with even small lies—as a 2006 study by Weiss and Feldman shows is often the case—who is this person with supposed shared personal interests that an employer believes they are hiring?

"Managers are often not self-aware of the illogical shortcuts they make in thinking that they like a person because of some inexplicable X factor that will contribute well to the team," says Ofer Sharone, assistant professor of sociology at the University of Massachusetts Amherst. He asserts that in doing so, they sabotage the company's interests by ignoring merit and not recruiting the most talented candidates. And, due to our tendency to gravitate toward those most similar to us, this helps create a less equitable society. Furthermore, as Rivera cites, many studies find that "for jobs involving complex decisions and creativity, more diverse teams outperform less diverse ones. Too much similarity can lead to teams that are overconfident, ignore vital information, and make poor (or even unethical) decisions."

As an alternative to vague behavioral questions, nonsensical brain teasers or discussions about favorite sports teams that bear little or no relation to the job

at hand, Sharone advocates assigning actual simulations during interviews. "Audition-based testing can play a larger role at earlier stages so that you're ultimately not forcing anyone to hire blindly, but you've changed the pipeline in a way that's much more fair," he says. As a positive example, he points to the Boston Symphony Orchestra which, in 1952, pioneered auditioning musicians blindly, leading to a sizable increase in the number of women selected. Today, companies like interviewing.io are using new technology to similar ends by anonymizing candidates' voices, changing the experience of at least long-distance interviewing.

When speaking with the website *goop*, Adam Grant, professor of psychology and management at the Wharton School of Business, commended the design firm IDEO for the way it fosters diversity by hiring for "cultural contribution." Rather than restrict its hiring pool to designers, it employs screenwriters and filmmakers to meet their need for writing narratives and anthropologists who help refine problem-solving methods as the company navigates new environments. In this approach to hiring, Grant echoes Celia de Anca, Director of the Centre for Diversity in Global Management at Madrid's IE Business School, who urges that companies should not stop at satisfying a diversity of origin (sex, race, etc.) but also hire for a diversity of personalities and aspirations between equals. "Eliminate some barriers of entry first through recruiting in social media and LinkedIn, among other means of global outreach," she says. "But after hiring, companies should value their employees' differences and the unique ways with which they each look at the world and approach their work."

Working Lives

First published in 1979, the book 'Working Cats' documents the cats that earn their keep.

# of Cats

Photographs by Terry deRoy Gruber

NEW JERSEY
PUBLIC
TELEVISION
1978
ANNUAL
REPORT

NEW JERSEY
PUBLIC
TELEVISION
1978
ANNUAL
REPORT

TAPE A

TAPE B

PREVIEW

CAM 3

TELEX

S-1800

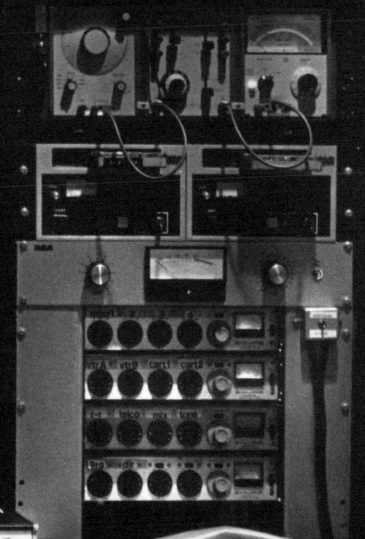

From wig shops to Italian restaurants and the back of taxicabs, cats are no strangers to the working world.
Above: Max holds down a nine to five at a tri-state art gallery.

Working Cats is photographer Terry deRoy Gruber's first book on cats; he has since published *Fat Cats* and *Cat High: The Yearbook*.
Above: J.P.'s career has taken him to the New York Stock Exchange.

To find working cats, Gruber ran ads in several publications seeking pets adopted by businesses and shops.
Above: Devo is a full-time local radio station star.

4

Directory

Science writer *Philip Ball* explains what happens when we see a pattern and why — even when there is no pattern to see—our brain will often establish one anyway.

JULIE CIRELLI

Pattern & Repetition

How do we perceive patterns in the shapes and colors around us, and why is it human nature to crave order—with a healthy dose of disorder—in our surroundings? Science writer Philip Ball has penned numerous books on the symbiotic relationship between the mind, the eye and the patterns in our built and natural world. Here, he explains how our minds recognize patterns and why we seek order amid chaos.

How many times does a motif have to repeat for the eye to recognize it as a pattern? This is a fundamental question for science: How many times does something have to recur before we suspect that we're seeing a law of nature and not just a coincidence? There's no definitive answer to the question because it has to do with our intuition about what we see—the impression that there's some order to the world around us. That intuition is so strong that we're prone to seeing pattern even when there's none. And we can discern genuine order even in shapes that have no repeating pattern at all, like a tree: It may look sort of random, but I suspect we sense the deeper regularity whereby the same basic form repeats at increasingly smaller scales as we go from trunk to branch tip.

What kind of behind-the-scenes mental gymnastics is the brain doing to help us understand what we're seeing when we recognize a pattern? When we see pretty much any scene—natural or otherwise—we're getting an overwhelming amount of visual information. We need to make sense of this information in order to navigate our way around the world. So our minds unconsciously make a best guess. This means,

for example, that we assume that there's continuity even when we can't actually see it—that the airplane that disappeared into a cloud is the same one that came out the other side, and that it traveled in a straight line in between. This sounds trivially obvious, but we have to do a lot of it—not least because our view of some objects is always partial, blocked by bits of others. Our brains very quickly learn rules for grouping objects together in our visual field. These rules were deduced in the early 20th century by a group of psychologists in Vienna who were called the Gestalt psychologists. They found that we group objects if they are the same shape, or the same color, or close together, or the same size. It's in this way that we see a series of stripes, not just as "one stripe... and another one... uh, and another..." but as a "striped pattern."

Is there an evolutionary benefit to simplifying the world around us? These grouping mechanisms are just what the brain does—we don't actually know if some of them are hardwired or learned. They are a best guess that allows us to make predictions about our environment and therefore they do have an evolutionary benefit. This is where our sense of pattern comes from, and it also partially explains why we find patterns pleasing: If there's an adaptive advantage to being able to spot them, then it makes sense that we will have evolved a neural "reward system" that makes us feel good when we do. Exactly the same kind of thing happens, by the way, for sound input, and this is why we can make sense of the incredibly complex sound signal that is music, and why it gives us immense pleasure. Music is actually a very

good analogy for vision in showing that we are inherently pattern-seeking creatures.

What about in our homes—is the human tendency to inflict order on our surroundings part of this need to group things by color and pattern? Everyone has a different threshold for how much pattern and order they seek, as well as a somewhat different view of what counts as "order." But these differences lie on a spectrum between simplicity—think minimalism—and complexity, which would be a polite way of describing my study. Somewhere on that spectrum each of us finds a compromise we can live with.

Does it calm the brain to surround ourselves with pared-down, predictable patterns? Or do we need some degree of disorder and discord, too? We do seem to find comfort in regularity. But it's worth noting that most patterns that we create or seek out aren't the simplest possible, but usually a bit more complex. Think of wallpaper designs: They're regular (they have to be, in order to be printed), but the patterned elements can be quite complex, not just squares or lines.

Hypothetically speaking, if our environments were totally minimized into white spaces and grids, would this be soothing for the brain or crazy-making? It has generally been found that for all kinds of stimuli—including art and music, as well as in our homes—people tend to prefer some kind of compromise. This reflects a feature of the human brain: There's an ideal level of stimulation that pleases us most. Too little and we're bored; too much and we're confused.

PATTERNS
by Peter Koepke

Containing more than seven million pattern samples, the Design Library in New York is the world's largest physical archive of textiles, swatches, wallpapers, embroideries, pattern books and production records from the 1750s to the present. A new book, *Patterns: Inside the Design Library*, presents highlights from the library's archive, with patterns that run the gamut from chintz, floral and modernist to "chaos," "bling," "insects" and "kaleidoscope." "The history of patterns is as broad and varied as that of music or literature," says library director Peter Koepke. "Patterns not only reflect their original time and place, but they often return and reappear."

Acclaimed Japanese artist *Hiroshi Sugimoto* discusses his new work on the self-inflicted demise of humanity.

DANIELLE DEMETRIOU

Breathing Space

The work of New York–based Japanese artist Hiroshi Sugimoto transcends the spatial boundaries of a single art form. He is best known for his minimal monochrome photography shot with a large-format camera. These intensely detailed images depict subjects ranging from seascapes and movie theaters to natural history dioramas.

However, Sugimoto's work is not confined to photographic expression. Architecture, art installations and theater direction all play a role in his four-decade-long meditation on the passage of time and interpretations of place. This is reflected in his recent work, *Lost Human Genetic Archive*. The antithesis of minimalism, the artwork charts the self-inflicted demise of humanity. It was first shown at the Palais de Tokyo in Paris in 2014 and more recently at the Tokyo Photographic Art Museum. Epically detailed and surprisingly humorous, *Lost Human Genetic Archive* is a jigsaw puzzle of rare artifacts, fossils, everyday items, handwritten texts and photography. Instead of a white gallery, the work is surrounded by walls of rusted corrugated iron, floors of pebbles and old wooden memorial boards from Japanese cemeteries. "The context of my work is always very important to me," Sugimoto says. "These materials contextualize everything—they show the passage of time and their own history."

DIARY OF A NOSE
by Jean-Claude Ellena

Known as "the nose," Jean-Claude Ellena kept a diary documenting his process as principal parfumeur at Hermès. Here, he ruminates on creating resonance in scent. "I remember that when the painter Émile Bernard described how Paul Cézanne approached watercolors, he came up with this idea: 'His method was unique, quite outside the usual technique and excessively complicated. He started with painting shadows and with an area of color that he covered with a second, larger one, then a third, until all these colors screening each other modelled the object by coloring it.' If you look closely at Cézanne's watercolors you can see that the areas of color do not completely cover each other, but are mostly juxtaposed. Their interplay creates a remarkable harmony. I proceed in a similar fashion when "modelling" a perfume, by freeing myself from the mind-set of proportions that I could have chosen—the wiser from previous experience—and by thinking only about the raw materials. It is the raw materials that shape a perfume; when they are juxtaposed, they set up resonances. When I try to establish harmony, the proportions establish themselves." *From* The Diary of a Nose: A Year in the Life of a Parfumeur *by Jean-Claude Ellena.*

Left photograph: Mikkel Mortensen, Prop styling: Atelier CPH. Right photograph: Guido Harari

RACHEL GALLAHER

This Woman's Work

In his latest book, *The Kate Inside*, Italian photographer *Guido Harari* presents the audacious spirit and restless creativity of iconic singer *Kate Bush*.

Like many twentysomethings in the 1980s, British musician Kate Bush was bold. But unlike the rebellious kids soaking up the zeitgeist by proxy through parties, concerts and radio waves, Bush spent her post-teen years making a creative mark on the independent music scene.

Catching early attention for her eclectic musical style and high-pitched soprano, the singer signed with EMI Records in 1976, releasing her first album, *The Kick Inside*, when she was just 19. Despite her age, Bush insisted on having strong creative control in all decisions affecting her music—a demand that continued as she catapulted to superstardom in the early '80s.

Three decades later, Bush has set a standard against which independent artists—women, particularly—are measured today. Her fearless personality shines through in the new book from rock photographer Guido Harari.

Unfolding like a scrapbook, *The Kate Inside* features more than 300 official photos, outtakes, Polaroids and candid shots of Bush taken by Harari between 1982 and 1993 while the singer recorded three different albums (*Hounds of Love*, *The Sensual World* and *The Red Shoes*) and made the musical short film *The Line, the Cross & the Curve*.

During this pivotal time in Bush's life, she broke free from commercial expectations and pushed creative boundaries by experimenting with musical styles and penning controversial lyrics. Page after page of *The Kate Inside* reveals a strong mix of fierceness and femininity underscored with self-assurance. From sensual shots to quiet moments caught in the studio, Harari freezes a period of time that, despite its '80s aesthetic, feels timeless. Perhaps it's the rebelliousness of youth or the complex mix of human emotion in each shot, but it's clear that there is a little bit of Kate inside us all.

From internment to avant-garde art institute: the rare life story of *Ruth Asawa*, the "fountain lady" of San Francisco.

SUZANNE SNIDER

Ruth Asawa

Ruth Asawa is best known for her sculptures "crocheted" from metal wire, figures she described as "drawings in space." Suspended, her voluminous forms have the unlikely appearance of fragile webs. The wire sculptures marry her art and craft training: high concepts from her time at Black Mountain College—the experimental art school-cum-farm in North Carolina that offered no degrees—merged with metal basket-making techniques that she learned in Mexico.

Despite critics' gendered readings of her art as craft, she flourished as an exhibiting artist. After three years at Black Mountain College, where Josef Albers and Buckminster Fuller were both mentors, she moved to San Francisco in 1949. There, she expanded into additional roles as an arts advocate, educator and mother. (She had six children in nine years with husband Albert Lanier.) In the 1950s, her work was shown at numerous museums including the Whitney and as part of the São Paulo Art Biennial. She was selected for public commissions in San Francisco, creating the famous mermaid fountain in Ghirardelli Square (1968) and the Hyatt Fountain (1973), which she designed collaboratively with public school children and her mother.

At home, her children were a constant part of her studio practice and the family ate dinner together every night as a rule. Her daughter Aiko recalls how "… if we really wanted to talk to her, we got one of the dowels and we'd start coiling wire for her, so that we'd be helping her and having a conversation with her." Asawa successfully fought for art education in public schools and was named to the San Francisco Arts Commission in 1968. She eventually served on President Carter's commission on mental health and the National Endowment for the Arts.

Asawa advocated for art programming but also embraced young children as collaborators well before "social practice" was in vogue. Her efforts toward social reform were fueled by her identity as an artist rather than an activist. She explained in an oral history, "Activism is wasteful. And it's better to be working on an idea. And building on that than to be breaking down and protesting something that exists," an idea that echoed Buckminster Fuller's critique at Black Mountain College.

Asawa was steadfast in her commitment to live and die making art. Asked by one interviewer in the 1970s, "How does an artist make a living these days?" Asawa replied, "Well, I've never held a job, so I would just do my own work. If I sell something, I sell something; if I don't, then I don't. If I don't sell too much, then I grow more in my vegetable garden and live on less […]" While Asawa could have easily joined the lecture circuit she politely declined, saying, "I'd rather be less sure and really explore things that I need to explore artistically, than to do that."

Born in 1926 to Japanese farmers in Southern California, Asawa was interned during World War Two with her family at age 16 (her father was moved to a separate location). After three years in two camps, Asawa attended Milwaukee State Teachers College but did not get a degree; no one welcomed a Japanese-American student teacher. Instead, she spent a summer in Mexico with one of her sisters and then moved to Black Mountain College, where the student body operated like a collective, each student assuming a role on the working farm in addition to their studies. She attended for three years (1946-1949) on a scholarship. As her BMC farm job, she churned butter.

Though Josef Albers, known for his flamboyant teaching style and treatises on color, was not an obvious influence on her sculpture, he was an undeniable influence on her worldview, offering the act of problem-solving as the heart of art making and living: "[Albers] presents a problem and then each one of us comes with a solution and we discuss all of the solutions and each one of us goes back with those seven or eight solutions […] so that each one of us has to be responsible for thinking for ourselves […] It means that it opens up new options."

In an oral history, Asawa explained her lifelong resistance of victimhood. "Even when [Milwaukee] ejected me. Then I said, 'Well, I'll go elsewhere.'" About the first internment camp, she said, "We really had a good time, actually. I enjoyed it," explaining that three Disney artists, also interned, offered art lessons in the track's bleachers, five hours a day. It was the first time that Asawa was freed from farm chores to make art.

Ruth Asawa died in 2013 and many critics have theorized without consensus about why her work is finding such an expanded audience posthumously. At a Christie's auction in 2013, a sculpture sold for $1.4 million, four times the appraised value. Of course, money meant little to Asawa. An expert in reframing her practice and her narrative, she explained: "We lived pretty poor and pretty hard. And […] we refused to acknowledge that we were poor. And that's very important. If you start acknowledging it then pretty soon you are. […] We gave up necessities so we could afford luxuries." When she was asked what kind of luxuries she bought, she answered "art supplies."

HOW TO MAKE DOUGH
by Ruth Asawa

Ruth Asawa expanded the reach of art-making with clear instructions and accessible materials. Most famously, she fine-tuned a dough recipe that called for just flour, salt and water. When baked, salt dough sculptures could be glazed or even cast in bronze. Asawa used the dough to make her own work and to collaborate with young people on commissions, such as the Hyatt Fountain. In the 1960s, she held a "dough-in" in Hawaii with 600 participants over three days. Here is the recipe:

4 cups flour
1 cup salt
1 ½ cups water

Mix the flour and salt. Add the water. Knead the dough until smooth. It might take up to 5 minutes of kneading to get the flour, salt and water properly mixed. This dough is not elastic, like bread dough. It should be soft, but still firm, and be able to hold the shape of a good mound. It doesn't like to be kneaded too much. When you attach two pieces of the dough together (such as adding arms to a body or eyes to a face), you should use very little water (lick it with your tongue, or dip your finger in water and dab on the water) before joining the dough together. Then give it a firm press. This will make a better bond when baking. After shaping your figures, bake on a tray or cookie sheet in an oven on low heat (250-325 F) until hard. The length of time depends on the thickness of your objects.

Sometimes a name tells you everything you need to know. Sometimes, as this occupationally themed puzzle demonstrates, it does the opposite.

MOLLY YOUNG

Crossword

ACROSS

1. Totals
5. The Jackson 5 hairdos
10. Scoundrel
13. Region
14. Slanted
16. Plastic ___ Band
17. Deer-slaying actress?
19. Vietnam Veterans Memorial artist Maya ___
20. Torrent
21. Prefix meaning "half"
22. Massive Australian bird
23. Toothy instruments
26. Alternative to dial-up, briefly
27. "___ Sounds" (Beach Boys album)
28. One time around the track
31. Dangerous kind of tide
32. Lavatory in London
34. In the mode of
35. See 51-Across
38. Bender
41. Speck of dust
43. Nation where bibimbap comes from
45. "Mr. Roboto" band
46. Dish you might find in a lab
48. Close
49. Historical period
50. US government agency in charge of taxation
51. With 35-Across, soup-stirring CEO?
53. Michael Stipe band
54. Clothes once known as "mogul's breeches"
56. Prefix with Norse, Vic, or Testament
59. Novelist Bellow
61. *Cogito ergo* ___
62. A dripping faucet or a hole in the roof, for example
64. The opposite of tight
68. "The Greatest" of boxing
69. Mitten-making actor?
72. Rent
73. Revere
74. Units of butter
75. Speedometer letters, in the US
76. Adolescents
77. Part of a Venetian blind

DOWN

1. Contented sounds
2. Wee bit
3. "The Hurdy-Gurdy Player" painter Georges _____ Tour
4. Adds seasoning, say
5. Like some trees and Wednesdays
6. Winter ailment
7. Wood and Howard
8. Chose
9. Appears to be
10. Luggage-toting composer?
11. "Spirited Away" genre
12. Homer Simpson's favorite breakfast item
15. What a dentist does before filling a cavity
18. Once around the sun
24. To convey by capillary action
25. Snuggle
28. Desk item that is also Pixar's mascot
29. Pliny the Elder called it "glutinous to a marvellous degree"
30. Metalworking songstress?
33. Photo ___ (political campaign events)
36. Raw mineral
37. "Ode on a Grecian Urn" poet
39. Brontë's "Jane ___"
40. Test
42. Make a mistake
44. Opera solo
47. Wagner's "Tristan und _____"
52. Ponder
54. Biblical song
55. Minty bourbon cocktail
57. Bare minimum
58. "The Divine Comedy" author
60. "I am looped in the ____ of her hair" (Yeats line)
63. Éric Rohmer film "Claire's ____"
65. Egg-shaped
66. "Go ___ Watchman" (most recent Harper Lee novel)
67. Prefix for "while"
70. Japanese currency
71. Baseball execs

Hans Ulrich Obrist

Kinfolk's contributing editor *Hans Ulrich Obrist* has turned curatorial work into a work of art in itself. Beyond his role as artistic director of the Serpentine Galleries, Obrist is a powerful figure on the exhibition circuit and has racked up thousands of hours' worth of interviews with artists along the way.

Illustration: Chidy Wayne

An admirable quality in others: Generosity
A good book: Journey to Mount Tamalpais by Etel Adnan
Your usual breakfast: Porridge
An underrated thinker: Édouard Glissant
A good habit of yours: Exercise
A bad habit: Coffee
A minor regret: Death is a dull fact, as Leon Golub once said
Your private refuge: Sils Maria, Switzerland
A necessary fiction: Robert Walser's Gazette Parisienne
Your hidden talent: Doodling
An outmoded fashion you appreciate: Handwriting

Stockists

A.P.C.
apc.fr

ACNE STUDIOS
acnestudios.com

ADÉLIE
adelie.dk

ANDREAS MURKUDIS
andreasmurkudis.com

BURBERRY
burberry.com

CÉLINE
celine.com

COMMON PROJECTS
commonprojects.com

COS
cosstores.com

CREATURES OF COMFORT
creaturesofcomfort.us

DAMIR DOMA
damirdoma.com

DOVER STREET MARKET
doverstreetmarket.com

FILIPPA K
filippa-k.com

FRAMA
framacph.com

HAKUÏ
hakui-shop.com

HARVEY NICHOLS
harveynichols.com

HAY
hay.dk

HENRIK VIBSKOV
henrikvibskov.com

HERMÈS
hermes.com

ISABEL MARANT
isabelmarant.com

ISSEY MIYAKE
isseymiyake.com

KÄHLER
kahlerdesign.com

LANVIN
lanvin.com

LEMAIRE
lemaire.fr

LIBERTY
libertylondon.com

LOEWE
loewe.com

LUISAVIAROMA
luisaviaroma.com

MAISON MARGIELA
maisonmargiela.com

MARCELO BURLON
marceloburlon.eu

MARGARET HOWELL
margarethowell.co.uk

MARYAM NASSIR ZADEH
mnzstore.com

MR. LARKIN
mrlarkin.net

MYKITA
mykita.com

NITTY GRITTY
nittygrittystore.com

NUANCE
nuance-scandinavia.com

OKI-NI
oki-ni.com

OLIVER PEOPLES
oliverpeoples.com

OPENING CEREMONY
openingceremony.com

PAUL SMITH
paulsmith.co.uk

PERRET SCHAAD
perretschaad.com

RAF SIMONS
rafsimons.com

RODEBJER
rodebjer.com

SAINT LAURENT
ysl.com

SAMUJI
samuji.com

SANDRO
sandro-paris.com

SEA NEW YORK
sea-ny.com

STELLA MCCARTNEY
stellamccartney.com

STEVEN ALAN
stevenalan.com

STILLEBEN
stilleben.dk

TIGER OF SWEDEN
tigerofsweden.com

TOAST
toa.st

TONSURE
tonsure.eu

TOTÊME
toteme-nyc.com

VALEXTRA
valextra.com

WON HUNDRED
wonhundred.com

WOOYOUNGMI
wooyoungmi.com

YOHJI YAMAMOTO
yohjiyamamoto.co.jp

ZEGNA
zegna.com

Credits

COVER
Photograph
Hasse Nielsen

Styling
Carolyne Rapp

Styling Assistant
Maria Rocha

Hair
Mette Thorsgaard

Hair Assistant
Hanna Söderblom

Model
Eddie Klint at Unique Models

P.37
Hair
Gavin Anesbury

Makeup
Justine Purdue

P.38
Makeup
*Jeannette Grønborg
Svendsen*

Styling Assistant
Celine Stene Syverud

Photography Assistant
*Frederik Ravn Rønne
Kastrupsen*

Model
*Anoucka at Elite Model
Management*

P.39
Styling Assistant
Emma Nyboe

Hair and Makeup
Marie Thomsen

P.43
Hair and Makeup
Abibat Durosimi

P.45
Products
Ring Chair by Bower

Retouching
Tomika Davis

P.47 — P.48
Hair and Makeup
Ignacio Alonso

Photography Assistant
Dominic Hedgecock

Photography Assistant
Rasmus Ståhl

Photography Assistant
Ellen Nykvist

P78 — P.81
Excerpted with permission
of the publisher *John Wiley
& Sons, Ltd*, from *The Eyes of
the Skin: Architecture and the
Senses* 3e Copyright © 2012
by Pallasmaa.

P82 — 99
Styling Assistant
Maria Rocha

Hair
Mette Thorsgaard

Hair Assistant
Hanna Söderblom

Model
*Eddie Klint at Unique Models,
Copenhagen*

Location
Blink Production

P.100 — 112
Hair and Makeup
Marie Thomsen

P.101
Artworks
*Vilhelm Hammershøi
at Ordrupgaard*

P.114 — P.131
Hair
Jerome Cultrera

Makeup
Bryan Zaragoza

Casting Director
Sarah Bunter

Models
*Christina C and Phoenix
at Wilhelmina Model
Management*

P.136 — P.145
Production
Frank Visser

P.148 — 152
Photography Assistant
Katrín Ólafsdóttir

P.156 — P.163
Styling
Emily Whitmore

Photography Assistant
Gwen Trannoy

SPECIAL THANKS
*Cristal Cardone
Sofia Di Leva
Julien Desselle
Dana Martin
Wolfgang & Ursula Frei
Edward Quinn Archive
Jakob Fibiger Andreasen
Christina Neustrup
Sara Hatla Krogsgaard
Brooke McClelland
Emma Bal
Priscilla Granozio
The Estate of Ruth Asawa*